Book Availability and the Library User

Book Availability and the Library User

MICHAEL K. BUCKLAND

Assistant Director for Technical Services, Purdue University Libraries, Lafayette, Ind.

PERGAMON PRESS INC.

New York · Toronto · Oxford · Sydney · Braunschweig

PERGAMON PRESS INC.
Maxwell House, Fairview Park, Elmsford, N.Y. 10523

PERGAMON OF CANADA LTD.
207 Queen's Quay West, Toronto 117, Ontario

PERGAMON PRESS LTD.
Headington Hill Hall, Oxford

PERGAMON PRESS (AUST.) PTY. LTD.
Rushcutters Bay, Sydney, N.S.W.

PERGAMON GmbH
Burgplatz 1, Braunschweig

Library of Congress Cataloging in Publication Data

Buckland, Michael Keeble.
Book availability and the library user.

"Based on a dissertation submitted to the University
of Sheffield."
Bibliography: p.
1. Libraries and readers. I. Title.
Z711.B923 1975   025.5   74-8682
ISBN 0-08-017709-3
ISBN 0-08-018160-0 (pbk.)

Printed in the United States of America

Dedicated to

A. Graham Mackenzie

and

Anthony Hindle

without whose leadership this book could not have been written

Contents

The Author

Michael K. Buckland is Assistant Director for Technical Services, Purdue University Libraries, West Lafayette, Indiana. His principal professional interests are library management and the application of research to library problems.

He entered library work as a trainee in the Bodleian Library of Oxford University, after studying history at that university. After taking his professional qualification in librarianship from the University of Sheffield, he joined the library staff of the University of Lancaster with primarily bibliographical duties. From 1967 to 1972 he was responsible on a day-to-day basis for the University of Lancaster Library Research Unit where a series of studies were undertaken concerning bibliometrics, book availability and library management games. Meanwhile he received a Ph.D. from the University of Sheffield.

His present responsibilities at Purdue include supervision of technical processing, automation and research. His publications include various technical reports, numerous professional papers and co-editorship of a forthcoming *Reader in Operations Research for Libraries.*

Preface

The essentially logistical problem of making library books physically available when wanted by library users is central to librarianship. This book is a tentative attempt to provide a treatise on this problem. As such it has to deal with both theoretical analysis and the practicality of solutions. No apology is made for the attention devoted to theoretical analysis, because the author believes that a clear conceptual understanding of the factors involved is important for improved librarianship. The fact that analytical models are not always usable does not mean that the insight that can sometimes be derived from such analyses will not lead to a better understanding of the problems and, thereby, to improved library services.

An attempt has been made to draw widely on the available literature. Nevertheless, this treatise (if the rather grandiose term may be permitted) draws heavily on some of the work and experiences of the first five years, 1967–1971, of the Library Research Unit at the University of Lancaster, England. This has the advantage of actuality but it also pinpoints a paradox in research into library problems. To be respectable, research needs to be of general application—not localised. However, its practical validity can only be demonstrated by implementation in a particular situation. Therefore, generality can only be demonstrated by localised application. Perhaps the answer, beyond recognising this dilemma, is to emphasise the difference between the structure of the problem that probably is generally relevant and the details of implementation that may be local.

The text, like the ideas and discoveries, has evolved over the years.

Some parts of the text appeared in first form in the *University of Lancaster Library Occasional Papers* and various papers. The present text is based on a dissertation submitted to the University of Sheffield for the degree of Ph.D.

The author proudly acknowledges his indebtedness to his former colleagues at Lancaster: outstandingly, A. Graham Mackenzie, University Librarian; Anthony Hindle, Department of Operational Research; and Ian Woodburn, Department of Systems Engineering; but also several other members of the staff. The encouragement and financial assistance of the Office for Scientific and Technical Information, London, and the Council on Library Resources, Inc., Washington, have been most important to the Unit. A special acknowledgement is also due to Michael Howe, Division of Economic Analysis, and Herbert Schur, Postgraduate School of Librarianship and Information Science, both of the University of Sheffield. Substantial benefit was also derived from people kind enough to scrutinise various drafts of the text. These included Geoffrey Ford (now at Lancaster) and Miriam Drake, Oliver Dunn and Edwin Posey (all three of Purdue). Also, an anonymous review arranged by the publisher proved helpful. Beyond this the author readily acknowledges the substantial amount of encouragement, stimulation and correction he has received from numerous friends on both sides of the Atlantic.

West Lafayette, Indiana   MICHAEL K. BUCKLAND

Part One: Definition

CHAPTER 1

Introduction

A. SCOPE

Intellectual access to recorded information has, quite properly, been a major preoccupation of librarians. Its importance has been reflected in the effort devoted to the design and creation of bibliographies, catalogues, classification schemes, and other devices that help establish the existence of individual documents and their relevance to specific enquiries.

However, intellectual access needs to be accompanied by physical access if the documents are to be used. The essentially logistical problem of making books* available to library users has received far less attention in the literature of librarianship than has the discussion of intellectual access.

The problem of managing the physical availability of books—a topic sometimes referred to as library stock control—has many ramifications. In the pages that follow, attention is focused on a group of related decision areas that are central to the problem. These areas are concerned with deciding how much material should be acquired and in how many copies, how long it should be kept and how it should be managed while it is kept. Within this area there are two persistent concerns. First, there is the problem of defining workable performance measures. Even if the ultimate benefit to the individual user and to the community is difficult to assess, workable measures of service are needed. Second, there is the

*The terms 'book' and 'document' are used here and elsewhere (unless stated otherwise) as generic terms to include all library materials: monographs, serials, periodicals, newspapers and other formats.

problem of relating the various decisions to common bases of cost and service so that planning can at least be economical and consistent. Unfortunately, in current library practice very little attention is given to the definition (let alone the use) of measures of service. Also, the number of books acquired tends to have little basis in the objective assessment of readers' requirements; the effective regulation of borrowing (as opposed to recording the loans) is rather poorly understood; and investment in the acquisition of duplicate copies tends to be rather arbitrary. Nevertheless, progress in stock control can be and has been made. Three topics in particular have been receiving quite a bit of attention: compact storage, retirement to secondary storage, and, currently, the economics of relying on external back-up facilities as exemplified by the Center for Research Libraries in the United States and the British Library Lending Division (formerly the National Lending Library for Science and Technology) in the United Kingdom.

B.   ORGANISATION

This book attempts to clarify the main features of library stock control and to provide, for the first time, something approaching a general treatment of the topic. The text has been organised as a logical progression in the following stages.

Part One: Definition

Library stock control is defined and placed in context. The organisation of the book is explained. (Chapter 1.)

Part Two: How Many Titles Should a Library Have?

Optimal size can only be defined in relation to a given group of users in a given situation. This problem is examined in some detail. The two key variables of library acquisitions are:

—number of titles acquired
—length of time they are kept.

Analysis of user behaviour reveals laws of diminishing returns with respect to each of the variables. These laws are described and there is a detailed examination of their implications for library stock control. Much of this analysis is theoretical and the limitations of present knowledge are noted. (Chapter 2 and Appendix A.)

Part Three: How Can One Diagnose Faulty Control of Book Availability In a Library?

Techniques have been developed that permit the librarian to diagnose the extent to which users fail to find the books they want and to identify the chief causes of this failure. These techniques are described and one such study is described in detail. (Chapter 3.)

Part Four: How Can Book Availability in a Library be Improved?

Two problem areas diagnosed in the previous section are examined.

The first problem area relates to binding policies. Binding necessitates absence from the shelf. This absence causes frustration. A cost-benefit approach to alternative binding policies is presented, which compares the policies with respect to costs and to the minimisation of user frustration. This brief study exemplifies key features of library stock control. (Chapter 4.)

The second problem area relates to the impact of borrowing on the availability of books wanted by users. This appears to be the most important problem area in the control of a library's stock and requires detailed analysis of user behaviour, the effects of loan policies, the purchase of duplicate copies, and the interactions among these factors. This area is examined in detail and, as a case study, research at the University of Lancaster is described from the initial analysis of the problem, through the definition of measures of performance, the definition of relationships, the construction of models, data-collection, simulation, change of policy, implementation, and the analysis of impact. (Chapters 5–9 and Appendixes B and C.)

Part Five: Summary

Finally, there is a recapitulation and it is suggested that a synthesis of the preceding chapters provides a basis for a new approach to the economics of library provision. (Chapter 10.)

Although an evenly balanced overview is desirable, some topics have been given more attention than others. This unevenness derives from three considerations:

(i) The state-of-the-art is unevenly developed. For example, there has been a negligible amount of analysis of the dynamics of user response to changes in standards of service.*

(ii) Some topics need a longer and more careful exposition than others in order to describe them adequately. For example, the description of the binding problem in Chapter 4 is far more straightforward than the analysis of loan policies in Chapters 5–9. In the case of the diagnostic techniques in Chapter 3, it seemed best to provide only a brief summary and to refer readers to the definitive descriptions published elsewhere.

(iii) In addition, in order to reduce the scope of the book to more manageable proportions, three problem areas that could properly be regarded as aspects of library stock control have been excluded. Each of them has been fairly thoroughly treated elsewhere. These are book selection problems (e.g. Danton[65]), spatial aspects of book shelving (e.g. Leimkuhler[123,127]), and the decision whether or not to allow readers freedom of access to book stacks (e.g. Ceadel[165] and Ratcliffe[186]). Another topic that has been excluded is the use of photocopying as a substitute for loan. For legal and fiscal considerations on-demand photocopying does not appear to be a viable substitute for routine borrowing at the present time. However, whenever there is reference to reliance on interlibrary loan, the definition of interlibrary loan can be taken to include the possibility of receiving a photocopy in lieu of a loan of the original.

The title of this book *Book Availability and the Library User* reflects a deliberate emphasis. The main thrust has been to try to relate acquisition, duplication, binding, circulation and discarding to the needs and behaviour of library users. Since a large amount of the demand for books tends to be concentrated on a small proportion of the library's stock, this emphasis is revealed in the attention devoted to the problems of managing the titles that are in relatively high demand. This can be seen as a shift in emphasis in comparison with earlier American studies in library stock control, which tend to stress the problems of storage, as revealed in the

*The project entitled *Fundamental research into factors affecting the use of library services* funded by the Council on Library Resources, Inc. (Grant 505) at the Lancaster Library Research Unit is one attempt to fill the gap. As of November 1973 the results have not yet been published. However, the publication during 1974 is projected of a report provisionally cited as: BRETT, V. M. and others. *The academic library: a systems view.* (University of Lancaster Library Occasional Papers, 8). Lancaster, England, University Library. Forthcoming ISBN 0 901699 233.

attention given in those studies to titles that are *least* used and to space-saving storage arrangements. The difference between these 'space-oriented' studies and the present 'user-oriented' attempt to relate stock control more directly to standards of availability is more a matter of emphasis than substance. Anyone interested in storage problems or in exploring the problems of library stock control more fully ought certainly to examine these earlier studies as well. Noteworthy examples include Grieder's article 'The effect of book storage on circulation service'[88]; the classic study by Fussler and Simon: *Patterns in the use of books in large research libraries* (1961, reissued by Chicago U.P., 1969)[80], and W. C. Lister's thesis *Least cost decision rules for the selection of library materials for compact storage* (PB 174 441)[133]. Others may be found in the Bibliography.

Finally, it should be observed that no attempt has been made to adopt or adapt the substantial literature on industrial stock control and inventory theory, beyond a limited amount of use of the mathematical theory of queues. Instead, library stock control has been examined afresh in the pages that follow.

Part Two: How Many Titles Should a Library Have?

CHAPTER 2

The Stock for an Individual Library

INTRODUCTION

The size of a library is determined by two factors: How many titles are bought and how long titles are kept.

In any given situation, the librarian is naturally apt to start by buying the books most needed by the group of users that he serves. The more books that can be bought the better. Since purchasing naturally begins with the books most likely to be in demand, it follows that each successive increment of annual expenditure will be devoted to successively less useful books. The marginal benefit of increased expenditure on books will never reach zero but, intuitively, there must be a law of diminishing returns and even if the marginal benefit never quite disappears, there are always alternative uses for library funds. Increased investment in *other* library services or investment *outside* the library must become preferable at some stage. In brief, there must be a law of diminishing returns if only it can be identified.

The second factor determining library size is the length of time that titles are kept. Space and, therefore, storage cost money and the cost of keeping a book depends on its physical size and not on its usefulness. Therefore, investment in the storage of useful books is clearly better in economic terms than the storage of less useful books. If there is a tendency for books to be used less and less, then the returns on the investment in continued storage must diminish. Although the benefit of keeping a book is unlikely to quite reach zero, there are always rival claims on a library's budget and at some stage increased expenditure on some *other* library service can be expected to become preferable. Here again a law of diminishing returns needs to be identified. The next two sections of this chapter are devoted to the identification and examination of these laws of diminishing returns. Section C contains a series of analyses of the implications of these laws in the context of collections of journals for which the empirical evidence is best established. Monograph* collections could be treated in a similar manner.

A. OBSOLESCENCE: THE VARIATION IN DEMAND FOR A TITLE THROUGH TIME

Library usage is characterised by chronological rhythms. In terms of total usage this is evidenced by daily, weekly and seasonal patterns. In a university context, there may also be evidence of the effect of lecture time-tables, bus time-tables and, of course, the change from term to vacation.

The distinction has been made by Line[131], Brookes[32] and others between the 'general' or worldwide use of the literature of a given subject by all users and 'local' use of the documents in a particular library. It is clearly the latter that is relevant to library stock control.

Very little study has been done on the short-term pattern of demand for individual titles, apart from results that are presented in Chapter 5. Almost all work has concentrated on the variation in usage from year to year, which is much more relevant to the purpose of the present chapter. It has been found consistently that the annual usage of books declines with age in a negative exponential pattern. Numerous studies of this 'obsolescence' have been reported. Commonly they are concerned with the periodical literature of a defined subject.

Although a negative exponential pattern of obsolescence is generally accepted for both monographs and periodicals, rigorous analysis becomes very difficult for reasons that are stressed in Brookes'[32] lucid treatment of obsolescence and also by Fussler and Simon[80].

There are two views of obsolescence:

(a) In a *diachronous* view, one is concerned with the use of a given document in successive years—'through time'.
(b) In a *synchronous* view, one is concerned with distribution of use made during a given span of time of documents of different ages.

*The term 'monograph' is used throughout to denote books in the narrower sense—publications that are not serials.

The complexities derive from the dynamic nature of the factors involved and the difficulties of identifying their effects on measurable data.

For example, an increase in the size of the user population served or in the intensity of use per user will result in an increase in the average use of books, unless the growth in demand is counteracted by a corresponding increase in the number of books. If the stock of books is increased without an increase in demand, then there will be a dilution of demand per book.

Furthermore, the age structure of the book stock may change. This will result in varying degrees of dilution for material acquired at different times. Similarly, the age structure of the pattern of demand may change. This would happen if there is a shift in emphasis from conventional scientific research towards research into the history of science requiring reference to historically important texts.

For library stock control 'general' obsolescence patterns offer little assistance. It is necessary to concentrate on the obsolescence of the use in the library concerned. A convenient approach is to adopt a synchronous view and treat the results as a probability distribution. This describes the manner in which current usage is distributed over material of various ages. It is convenient to distinguish the obsolescence distribution from the level of total demand in absolute terms because the distribution is likely to remain more stable than the level of demand. For example, the British Library Lending Division (formerly the National Lending Library for Science and Technology) has reported that usage of their books has been *increasing* with age diachronously.* A plausible explanation is that the *synchronous distribution* has probably remained a fairly stable negative exponential, but that for individual documents the decline through time in their *share* of total usage is nevertheless an increase in absolute terms because the decline in proportionate use has been more than compensated by the steep and steady rise in *total* demand. Except in very unstable situations, the combination of a synchronous probability distribution and a measure of total usage is likely to be the most practical way to handle the use of obsolescence data for prescriptive purposes and also for predictive purposes where stock control is based adaptively on the measured use of individual documents.

*Private communication.

B. SCATTERING: THE VARIATION IN DEMAND FROM TITLE TO TITLE

It is obvious that some books are used more than others. For every book in a library, there are thousands that the librarian has not seen fit to acquire because the expected usage is deemed too low. There may also be other titles that the librarian would like to acquire because they would be heavily used but which are unobtainable because they are out of print. Within every library there are books that have remained unused for years and others that are in heavy demand, even with waiting lists of would-be readers. Since this feature of library use is fundamental to library provision, it is important to analyse the nature of this variation in demand from title to title and to describe it in such a way as may be helpful in providing guidance in library planning.

Considerable progress has been made in the analysis and description of this variation, especially since 1967. Serials are particularly convenient to analyse in this manner because a title will normally continue in publication for a number of years. It is, therefore, convenient to compare the use of many different titles over the same period of years. Three methods have been used in this kind of analysis:

(i) The *literature of a subject* can be represented by a comprehensive list of articles on that subject. This list can be regarded as representing the literature needed by library users interested in that subject. Analysis of such a list will indicate which journals contain a large number of these articles and it can be presumed that these journals will be more useful to this group of users than journals that contain very few or none of the articles.

(ii) *Citations* in articles or books can be analysed on the assumption that an author will refer only to items useful for an understanding of his topic. The totality of such citations can, therefore, be regarded as an approximation to the useful literature of a subject as defined by the group of articles and books whose citations were analysed—commonly 'the ten leading journals on . . .'. Periodicals that are relatively heavily cited are likely to be more useful than those that are cited little or not at all.

(iii) *Actual usage* of items as recorded on a library's borrowing records, requisition slips or other records is more directly relevant to stock control in that it reflects the usage made of the stock of a library by its readers. Raisig has criticised this approach.[182] Certainly the data will lack details of items used inside the library, usage of copies personally owned or borrowed from other libraries or attempts to use items not found in the library. However, attempts to make explicit adjustments for these factors rapidly become unmanageable but they are unnecessary adjustments if one is concerned with measuring the actual demand on a library as opposed to measuring the cosmic importance of a given title.

It should be clearly admitted that all three methods of analysis measure different things. It is rash to assert that any one of them should be regarded as a measure in any absolute sense of the *usefulness* of titles to a group of library users. All three types of data can, however, be treated as approximate guides to the variations in usefulness of specific titles to different groups of users, even though all three methods are open to criticism on theoretical grounds. All three, however, are practical techniques and, what is, perhaps, more important, the literature available seems to suggest that all three give very similar results.

The pioneer of the analysis and description of the variation in demand from title to title was Dr. S. C. Bradford, then Librarian of the Science Museum Library in London. He examined the literature of applied geophysics and the literature of lubrication.[23,24]

In each case, he counted the number of references to each periodical title. This indicated the variation from title to title in each subject. He then ranked the titles according to their productivity (the number of references contributed by that periodical to the literature concerned) and created a description of each literature by drawing a graph showing the number of references contributed by the *single* most productive periodical, the number contributed jointly by the *two* most productive periodicals, the *three* most productive periodicals, the *four* . . . , and so on. Naturally, the additional number of references contributed by successively less productive periodicals became fewer and fewer. *However, Bradford noticed that this decreasing productivity followed a recognisable pattern* and since he had been writing in terms of the '*scattering*' of a literature over journal titles, this pattern came to be known as '*Bradford's Law of scattering*'. It is convenient to illustrate this pattern graphically. This is normally done by plotting the cumulative productivity vertically on an arithmetical scale and plotting the cumulative number of periodicals horizontally on a logarithmic scale. The result is invariably of the form given in Fig. 2.1. This graphical illustration (or 'bibliograph') of Bradford's Law of scattering reveals that for much of its length the relationship is linear, but that it is not linear at the extremes.

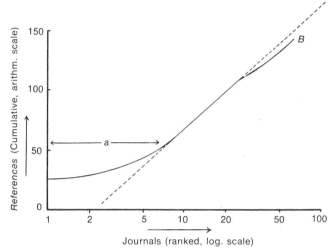

Fig. 2.1. A graphical representation of a typical example of the pattern found by Bradford when examining the scattering of a literature over different titles. (The data relate to English language articles on Boccaccio 1955–1968 and were kindly supplied by Mr. F. S. Stych.[209])

(i) Although the *most productive* few journals contribute most (by definition), their contribution tends to be less than the simple straight-line relationship would indicate. This is reflected as a curve in the line in what is called the 'nuclear zone' (a).

(ii) Commonly at the other end of the line, amongst the least productive journals there is a falling away from linearity. This feature is indicated by *B* and is known picturesquely as the 'Groos droop'.[30] Brookes has argued cogently that the 'Groos droop' may be symptomatic of malfunction in the system studied or inadequate data collection.[30] It should be stressed, however, that in the discussion of library stock control, the linear section is of most importance.

Bradford published a description of this pattern in 1934 in an article in *Engineering* entitled 'Sources of information on specific subjects'.[24] Although he republished it in his book *Documentation*[23] in 1948, it was not very widely known and appears to have been regarded mainly as a curiosity of subject bibliography until a flurry of interest from 1967 onwards. During this gap the main events were:

—a paper by Vickery in 1948 that clarified the mathematical formulation of this pattern,[222]

—papers by Kendall[111,112] in 1960 and 1961 that commented on the similarity between Bradford's finding and the work of G. K. Zipf[236],
—two seminal papers by Cole in 1962[61] and 1963[60] who collected data and related the results to considerations of library size, and
—writings by Fairthorne[73,75] who included Bradford's Law in his rigorous analyses of information retrieval.

C.   ANALYSES OF LIBRARY HOLDINGS OF JOURNALS—Part I

In 1967, staff at the University of Lancaster Library were attempting to deduce optimal strategies for the allocation of library resources by establishing play-offs between the marginal benefits of increasing expenditure in various directions. More specifically:

(i) Assuming that one knows how the use of books declines with age, one can estimate the benefit (and costs) of investing in continued retention of documents.

(ii) Assuming that one knows the chronological pattern of use of a given title one can estimate the benefits (and costs) of various binding policies: the time at which to bind is one parameter but the problem in mind was the extent to which it is justifiable to pay extra for a faster binding service, thereby reducing the frustration of readers who seek books that are away from the shelves.

While these two aspects were theoretically tractable, the open-ended problem that remained was that increased expenditure on longer retention or faster binding would in practice result in less money being available for other things—notably in a curtailment of the resources available for buying books. How could one estimate the loss of usefulness and relate it quantitatively to the investment in prolonged retention or faster binding? Intuitively, it must depend largely on the size of the book fund in relation to the demand made on the library. If money is very scarce, then a reduction of book purchasing is likely to be less acceptable than if there is plenty of money. In the latter case, increased investment in longer storage or faster binding would be at the expense of the least useful documents whose absence might hardly be noticed. What was clearly needed to complete the analysis was an explicit formulation of the law of diminishing returns with respect to increasing the range of titles held. The solution came with the realisation that this is precisely what Bradford's Law of scattering is: a law of diminishing returns with respect to the increase in the number of titles in a collection—always assuming that more useful titles are acquired before the less useful titles. Seen in this perspective, the pattern that Bradford perceived becomes not so much a statistical curiosity in subject bibliography as potentially an extremely powerful tool in the economic analysis of library provision.

Reference to the literature to find a mathematical formulation of Bradford's law showed that Cole[60] had recognised the relevance of Bradford's law to library stock control. Meanwhile, other researchers had been at work re-examining Bradford's work. Leimkuhler[122], at Purdue University, presented a reformulation of Bradford's law—and, thereby, helped to internationalise what had been a predominantly British contribution to librarianship. Brookes[29,30] at University College, London, also developed a new formulation of Bradford's law (calling it the 'Bradford–Zipf distribution') and has stressed the convenience of graphical as opposed to mathematical methods of using it. Since then, others also have joined the debate on the true nature* and correct derivation of Bradford's law, e.g. Fairthorne[74], Naranan[163,164], O'Neill[169] and Wilkinson[232].

Some examples will be given of the use of Bradford's Law of scattering and of obsolescence by examining stock control problems in the case of an imaginary library specialising in the literature of petroleum. These examples illustrate well the significance of Bradford's Law of scattering, the power of mathematical models and some of the limitations of both. Anyone interested in the mathematics involved will find a more detailed exposition of the same analysis, replete with equations, in Appendix A.

In the first section of sample analyses, it is assumed that all titles are retained for the same length of time before discarding.

C1. Potentially Most Useful Stock Pattern

Let us start with the simplest possible problem and assume that we are concerned with a library that can accommodate a limited number of volumes of periodicals. How many titles, retained for how many years would provide the most useful service? Let us assume, for simplicity, that all titles will be retained for the same length of time before being discarded. We must, of course, state what we mean by 'most useful'. A reasonable definition of 'most useful' (which we retain throughout this

---

*The best review is by Fairthorne[74], which largely supersedes Buckland and Hindle[48]. For speculation that scattering and obsolescence might be related see Buckland[44]—but also O'Neill[169].

chapter) is 'of maximal immediate availability'. In other words, the pattern of stock that meets more of the demand falling upon the library than would any other pattern of stock. The problems caused by lending and by the effect of duplication are considered in later chapters.

Returning to our imaginary petroleum library and assuming that it has a storage capacity of 2,000 volumes (and that we can define a volume as one year of one title), we can begin to explore alternative policies. At one theoretical extreme, one could postulate subscribing to 2,000 titles and retaining the parts for one year only before discarding. Such a policy would clearly include the titles of major interest, many titles of minor interest and, very likely, by the time one approaches the 2,000th title, material of very little interest indeed. The *range* of titles is very desirable. What would make the users of the library demand the resignation of the librarian would be the practice of discarding titles after one year. It would be far more useful to have immediate access to older parts of the more heavily used titles than to have the privilege of access to recent parts of the very rarely used titles. By using data on the pattern of obsolescence, one can estimate the proportion of demand that is for materials up to twelve months old and, thereby, assess the proportion of demand that this extreme policy could be expected to meet.

At the other theoretical extreme would be the policy of concentrating on one title and filling the shelves with a complete backfile of that title. This would often be practicable if one had space for only 20 volumes. It would be possible in a very few cases if one had space for only 200 volumes, but it would not be possible with space for 2,000 volumes. In a 2,000 volume library, any policy near this extreme would probably provide full availability with respect to a few of the most heavily used titles regardless of the age of the volume required. Nevertheless, the users of the library would certainly be highly dissatisfied because they would often want to refer to titles other than the few most used. Provided sufficient data were available, one could use Bradford's Law of scattering to calculate the proportion of demand that is concentrated on the few titles taken and how much falls on the other titles that are not taken. This would provide an estimate of the usefulness of this particular policy.

Since there is a law of diminishing returns with respect to the number of titles taken and also a law of diminishing returns with respect to the length of time the volumes are retained, one would expect the most useful solution to be a compromise between the two. Intuitively, one would not expect to choose either of the extreme policies defined above in which one or the other of the laws of diminishing returns is taken to its extreme.

In a petroleum library with a capacity of 2,000 volumes, one would expect that, for example, 200 titles each retained for 10 years to be a more useful policy than either of the extremes.

However, in order to compare alternative policies based on a restricted range of titles *and* a restricted retention period, then the calculations would have to involve *both* Bradford's Law of scattering *and* obsolescence. Using Cole's data on the pattern of journal usage in a petroleum library, it is possible to use published formulae concerning scattering and obsolescence to compare a continuous range of policies. In fact, the usefulness increases rapidly as one increases the number of titles acquired even though this involves discarding older volumes. Then there is a wide range of policies between which it is difficult to choose because the advantages of subscribing to an additional title tends to equal the disadvantages of a shorter retention time. Gradually as one approaches the extreme of very many titles kept for a very short time, these policies emerge as progressively less and less useful. This can be depicted graphically in Fig. 2.2.

Cole examined the imaginary case of a petroleum library that received 2,000 requests a year and can accommodate 2,000 volumes of journals.[60] He concluded that 190 titles, all retained for 11 years, would constitute the most useful stock pattern and that this would satisfy about 75% of the requests. It should be added that, in repeating Cole's approach, as described in Appendix A, it was found that in this particular case the results are not very sensitive to variations in the number of titles taken. Sixty more, or sixty fewer titles, with a corresponding adjustment to the

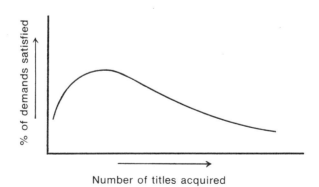

Number of titles acquired

Fig. 2.2.   Increase in the proportion of demands satisfied as the number of titles acquired increases.

retention period would make little difference to the number of requests satisfied by a collection of 2,000 volumes.

C2. Best Value for Money

In the analysis above, we were concerned with making the best use of limited space. A more practical question is how to make the best use of a limited amount of money. This is a different problem and consequently can be expected to have a different answer. The two costs in this example are taken to be acquisition costs and storage costs and we assume that there is a budget that is to be used for both.* How many titles, retained for how many years would provide the most useful service for a given budget? What is the best allocation of budget between acquisitions and storage?

Unlike the previous analysis, the cost of different policies will vary even for the same number of volumes because retaining a volume for an extra year will only increase the storage costs, but acquiring a volume by subscribing to an additional title will incur both a storage cost and also a subscription cost. This consideration creates an economic incentive to reduce the range of titles and increase the retention period. However, this reduction in costs has to be weighed against the change in usefulness that would result from having fewer titles and that would be partially but not completely compensated by longer retention of the titles acquired.

Furthermore, the optimal solution in any given situation will depend critically not only on the patterns of scattering and obsolescence and on the size of the budget, but also on the acquisition costs and the storage costs. For example, if two libraries had identical budgets and identical user-populations, one would *not* expect them to have identical collection policies if one was in a city with high storage costs and the other in a rural area with low storage costs. We can conveniently illustrate this analysis by calculating optimal policies for two imaginary petroleum libraries: one located where storage costs are high; the other where storage costs are low. The results, based on the models in Appendix A, are indicated in Table 2.1. Two features of these results deserve attention:

*In practice, fiscal conventions in libraries are not normally as simple as this. Nevertheless, both costs are real, substantial and have to be paid for somehow. The effects of fiscal conventions on the quality of managerial decision-making is an interesting topic but outside the scope of this book. Common conventions such as the non-transferability of monies, at least in the short term, between separate accounts for (i) salaries and wages, (ii) supplies and equipment, (iii) books and binding and the practice of not charging space costs to the library budget would seem to guarantee less than optimal allocation of resources.

(i) On account of the reduced storage costs, the rural library can afford to be substantially larger—more than 50% more volumes at each budget.

(ii) The benefits of increasing the collection through reduced storage costs or through an increased annual budget do not, in these particular examples, have much impact on the proportion of requests satisfied. In both cases, increasing the budget by 50% has resulted in roughly a 10% increase in the proportion of requests satisfied. This suggests that in these imaginary libraries the laws of diminishing returns are exercising a considerable effect already.

Table 2.1.

	City Library	Rural Library
Assumptions:		
Annual acquisition costs	£5 per title	£5 per title
Annual storage costs	£0·125 per volume	£0·033 per volume
Requests received	2,000 per annum	2,000 per annum
Optimal policies:		
Annual budget £1,000		
Titles taken	140	175
Retention period	18 years	22 years
Volumes in stock	2,520	3,850
Requests satisfied	76%	80%
Annual budget £1,500		
Titles taken	205	260
Retention period	18 years	23 years
Volumes in stock	3,690	5,980
Requests satisfied	83%	88%

C3. Optimal Binding Policies

Although binding policies are outside of the intended scope of this chapter, an analysis has been included here because it fits quite neatly into the series of analyses being presented.

In this analysis we assume that binding costs must be paid from the same budget as purchase and storage costs. The problem is to determine which combination of acquisition, binding and discarding policies will give the best value for any given budget. Setting aside considerations of the quality of binding, two key binding decisions are: (i) when to bind; and (ii) how far it is worth paying extra for faster binding:

(i) At first sight there is a good case for delaying binding for a while until the decline in the rate of usage, through obsolescence, makes the temporary absence of a volume from the shelves less inconvenient to the user. Indeed, this would argue for indefinite postponement—or, rather, not binding at all. Until the penalty for not binding and, more especially, the cost of delaying binding is better understood and measured, it does not seem possible to indicate mathematically whether material should or should not be bound—still less *when* it should be bound—though this probably is a tractable problem. In the following analysis, it is assumed that, as a matter of policy, titles *will* be bound. The average age of materials sent for binding can be varied and, consequently, the effects on the library's usefulness of prompt or delayed binding will also vary.

(ii) The second important question concerns the time taken to bind material. This is, in practice, the length of time that material is absent from the shelves. Although, in general, the cheapest binding rates will be chosen, there is always the possibility of choosing to pay a little extra for a more rapid service. How far would this be justifiable?*

The payment of extra money for speedier binding would be at the expense of the monies available for purchase or for storage—at the expense, in effect, of the size of the library. Intuitively, the decision ought to depend not only on the benefits of reduced absence from the shelves, but also on the lavishness of the budget itself. The larger the budget in relation to the users' needs, the greater the number of little-used volumes and the more easily some of these could be sacrificed for the benefits of prompter binding. The benefits of prompter binding, however, will depend on the time at which material is sent for binding. Because of the effects of obsolescence, the average number of demands per week on any given volume can be expected to decline. Consequently, the effects on user convenience of reducing the binding time from, say, five weeks to three weeks would be greater if all journals are bound as soon as volumes are completed than if volumes were bound when they are two years old.

Let us illustrate this dilemma by considering that the librarians of our two imaginary petroleum libraries had three options:

Binder A charges on average £1·10 per volume, but material is absent from the shelves for about three months.

---

*For the sake of exposition, this discussion assumes that the binder determines the binding time. This is not the whole story because the absence from the shelves does include the preparation before binding and verification and readying for the shelves after binding. These are activities performed by library staff and could, at a price, be made faster.

Binder B charges on average £1·25 per volume, but material is absent from the shelves for one month.

Binder C charges on average £1·50 per volume, but material is absent from the shelves for only about one week. (We assume one fiftieth of a year.)

Which binding policy would result in the most useful library service? We assume that all titles are retained for the same length of time before discarding and that all titles are sent to binding at the same average age. We can use obsolescence patterns to estimate the number of requests likely to be made for materials during binding, because the binding period is the span between the average age at which material is sent to binding and the average age at which material is returned and because obsolescence patterns can be used to estimate the proportion of usage that is before or after each given average age. The number of requests will, of course, depend both on the choice of age at which material is sent to binding *and* the length of the binding period.

This loss of usefulness and the costs associated with different binding policies can be related mathematically to the budget and also to the options concerning range of titles received and retention period. By means of data on scattering and obsolescence, all these variables can be meshed together algebraically to produce estimates that can be used to compare alternative policies.

By using the equations presented in Appendix A, we come to the same conclusion for both libraries for annual budgets of £1,000, £1,500 and £2,000. If the material is sent to binding at an average age of two years or less, then the choice of the quick but expensive Binder C would, by a very narrow margin, result in the most useful library service even though the substantially higher cost of binding means that marginally fewer titles can be bought and that those that are bought would be discarded slightly earlier. If, on the other hand, journals are sent for binding at an average age of five years, then the intensity of use will have diminished somewhat and with it the intensity of the inconvenience of slower binding. At this point, use of the slower, cheaper Binder B results in a very slightly more useful service.

D.   ANALYSES—Part II

Investigators of journal retention periods have generally tended to assume that all titles are to be retained for the same period of time (e.g. Cole[60], Hanson[94], Meadows[147] and others). This assumption has the great virtue of simplicity but, unless we are to deny the existence of scattering and obsolescence, it must necessarily lead to less than optimal results. This can be recognised by considering the actual distribution of usage over the volumes in a collection. Imagine for simplicity a collection of 10 titles, each retained for 10 years only. By definition, the least used title is used less than the most used title. For each title, the volume that is 10 years old tends to be used less than the latest volume. Combining these two considerations, we conclude that the 10-year-old volume of the least used journal is probably used considerably less than the 10-year-old volume of the most used journal. Intuitively, it seems likely that the 10-year-old volume of the least used journal is the least used volume in the collection and should probably be discarded in favour of keeping one more year of the most used journal or in favour of acquiring the current year's volume of another title not yet held. In other words, it would be a much more useful collection if we were to abandon the policy of retaining all titles for the same length of time and determine a discarding point *for each title*. This would result in retaining longer the volumes of the heavily used titles and discarding earlier the volumes of less used titles.

In this section, we shall examine some sample analyses that do *not* assume that all titles are retained for the same length of time. In these analyses, we shall determine an individual discarding age for each title; the more heavily used titles are kept longer than the less heavily used. As before, the mathematical details can be found in Appendix A. For simplicity, an average obsolescence rate is assumed for all titles in a given collection, but different obsolescence rates for different titles could be used if known.

D1. Potentially Most Useful Stock Pattern

Now that we have relaxed the assumption about retention times being the same, we can reconsider the earlier analysis C1. If we assume that a library can accommodate only a limited number of volumes, what combination of acquisition and discarding policies would be most useful? How many titles should be purchased and how long should each be retained?

Since the problem is to determine the *most useful* volumes, we would not wish to include a volume that satisfied, say, one request a year if it meant the exclusion of another volume that would have been used more than once a year. We should need, therefore, to observe the fall-off of use of each title and ensure that, at the discarding point of each, its usefulness was similar to that of the other titles. Otherwise the restriction on the number of volumes would mean that the over-prolonged retention of one title would cause the premature discarding of volumes that would have been more useful. In other words, *the optimal solution is when the marginal utility of further retention is the same for all titles.* Mathematically this is done by using the scattering formula to estimate the amount of demand falling on a given title and then the obsolescence formula to estimate the age by which usage of individual volumes will have declined to a particular threshold. This is the threshold (and, therefore, the age) at which the title should be discarded. The numerical value in demands per annum should be the same for all titles (though, of course, the age will vary from title to title). The numerical value of the threshold will have to be computed according to the circumstances (e.g. the scatter, the obsolescence, the budget, the demand, and the acquisition and storage costs) in order to give the desired policy. Fussler and Simon[80] arrived empirically at substantially the same decision rule for discarding volumes from the main library and 'retiring' them to a less accessible store.

> Several sets of rules were developed for separating serials into groups for storage on the basis of predicted future use. The rules that seem best are based on [a] system of surveying each serial title from the oldest volume onward, until one reaches volumes showing the specified amount of use. [cf. the threshold described above] These rules separate out large numbers of volumes that will show a relatively small amount of use in future years. (Fussler & Simon[80], p. 105. The words in brackets have been added.)

In analysis C1, we considered the case of a petroleum library with space for 2,000 volumes of journals to satisfy 2,000 requests. We found that if we accept the restriction that all titles are to be retained for the same length of time, then, at best, (with about 190 titles retained for about 11 years) we could expect to satisfy 75% of the requests. If, however, we can choose an individual discarding age for each title, then we can apply the strategy developed in the previous paragraph. We find that by acquiring 420 titles with retention periods varying from 1 to 23 years we can satisfy 80% of the requests with 2,000 volumes.

By means of a similar calculation, we could estimate that 75% of the requests could have been met with only 1,400 volumes provided that the titles were not all retained for the same period. The satisfying of 75% of the requests with 1,400 volumes instead of 2,000 (as in C1 above) constitutes a reduction of 600 volumes and deserves some comment.

(i) This 30% saving in library size is achieved because the stock policy has been changed to match more closely the pattern of users' behaviour as reflected by scattering and obsolescence.

(ii) The 30% saving in library size may not constitute a saving in library expenditure because although storage costs are reduced, the revised policy involves subscribing to many more titles that are kept for quite short periods. The cost of the additional subscriptions may more than compensate for the reduction in storage costs.

(iii) Assuming individual discarding points for each title, an increase in collection size from 1,400 to 2,000 would only increase the proportion of requests satisfied from 75% to 80%. The smallness of this increment in usefulness in spite of a very substantial increase in size reflects the combined effects of the two laws of diminishing returns.

D2. Optimal Library Size and Minimum Costs

As before, we now turn from the best use of space to the more practical question of how to make the best use of money. In analysis C2, we examined the optimal deployment of the budget with respect to acquisitions and storage. We will now return to this problem but take it one stage further and consider interlibrary loan as an alternative to local availability.

Assuming that the librarian will attempt to meet all demands, the budget will have to cover four costs:

(i) Cost of acquiring titles.
(ii) Cost of storing titles until discarding.
(iii) Interlibrary loan costs for borrowing items that the library has discarded.
(iv) Interlibrary loan costs for borrowing items that the library never acquired.

What combination of acquisition and discarding policies will minimise the sum of these four costs? Holding firmly to the goal of minimising costs, the first principle would be to retain volumes until their usage had declined to the point at which it was more expensive to store them than to incur the cost of an interlibrary loan on the infrequent occasions when anyone wanted that particular volume. This is relatively straightforward as a concept in the case of journals that are heavily used, but a complication arises with the less used titles. Consider, for example, a little used journal, that ought, on this principle, to be discarded after three years from acquisition. On a straight comparison of storage costs versus interlibrary loan costs, keeping this title for the first three years is cost-effective. However, this does not take into account the cost of *acquiring* the title and, if one did so, then it might well have been cheaper to have relied entirely on interlibrary loan and not to have acquired it at all. This composite policy could be defined as acquiring as many titles as possible and storing the volumes until reliance on interlibrary loan becomes cheaper than continued storage, provided that the combined cost of acquisition and storage for any given title is less than complete reliance on interlibrary loan.

This composite rule can now be applied to our imaginary petroleum library and, using the calculations described in Appendix A, we estimate that the following results (Table 2.2) constitute the least cost policy.

Table 2.2.

	City Library	Rural Library
Assumptions:		
Acquisition cost	£5 per title	£5 per title
Storage cost	£0·125 per volume	£0·03 per volume
Interlibrary loan cost	£1 per loan	£1 per loan
Conclusions:		
Titles	50	62
Retention range	11–24 years	16–30 years
Volumes in stock	744	1,230
Overall cost	£1,160 per annum	£1,095 per annum
Satisfaction from stock	58%	63%

D3. The Cost of Reducing Delays

In the previous analysis, the aim was to minimise the cost of providing a library service to meet a specified amount of demand. The choice between satisfying demand from stock and satisfying it by interlibrary loan was based solely on the basis of cost to the library. No account was taken of the fact that there is a delay involved in satisfaction by interlibrary loan. On the other hand, causing library users to wait is generally regarded as undesirable. No way appears to have been devised for objectively measuring the cost to be assigned to this delay. Nevertheless, it is possible to explore the cost to the librarian of reducing this delay.

One approach is to increase the size of the library. This will result in a reduction in the need for interlibrary loans and, therefore, in the *average* delay in finding material. This can be done by acquiring more titles that are rarely used and by retaining volumes longer before discarding them. In both cases, this would be a deliberate policy of moving beyond the point at which reliance on interlibrary loan would have been cheaper.

Consequently, both total costs and costs per usage will increase, slowly at first, but then more and more steeply. A graph of the total library costs in relation to the proportion of demand satisfied from stock is shown in Fig. 2.3.

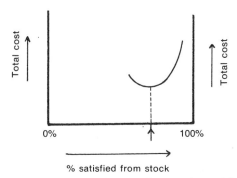

Fig. 2.3.   Relationship between total cost and proportion satisfied from stock.

It can be seen that total costs decrease as the stock increases up to a certain size. Then, as the laws of diminishing returns steadily reduce the benefits of additional titles and continued storage, continued expansion of the library becomes less economical than reliance on interlibrary loan. Total costs rise after the least cost solution, which is indicated by the arrow (↑).

However, increasing library size and decreasing reliance on interlibrary loan reduce the number of interlibrary loans and, therefore, the average delay in getting books into readers' hands. The problem is to achieve the optimal combination of speed of service and cost of service. If objective data were available on the cost to be associated with various speeds of service, then an optimal policy could be determined. In the absence of such data, the best that can be done is to try to assess the effects of any choice of library size on average delays and on service costs and to hope that better management information will lead to wiser management. The relationship between costs and delays is shown graphically in Fig. 2.4.

In this discussion, we have only considered the effect of increasing library size as a means of reducing delays. This is, of course, unrealistic. Even if interlibrary loans are being arranged as speedily as possible at any given unit cost, the delays can generally be reduced further at the cost of a rise in unit costs by the use of telex, telephone or telefacsimile, by

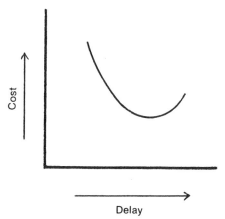

Fig. 2.4.   Relationship between cost and delay.

investing in better finding lists and union catalogues, by more or better staff, by investment in improved external lending facilities, and so on; in the extreme case one could dispatch the user to another library holding the required material. It remains to be determined in any given situation how far these factors could reduce delays more economically than by increasing the size of the library.

E.   MONOGRAPHS

In the preceding sections and in most writings on Bradford's Law of scattering and obsolescence, attention is confined implicitly or explicitly to serials. Although one may feel that the usage of monographs—and, therefore, stock policies—*ought* to follow the same sort of pattern, the analyses discussed above do not seem to be directly usable for monographs because a monograph title, unlike a serial title, is not a continuing publication. However, the problem is similar. Demand is unevenly distributed and much of it is concentrated on a small range of titles and it is convenient to have these available locally. Vast numbers are needed very infrequently and for these the librarian needs to arrange reasonably quick access. Both book budget and storage costs indicate selectivity in purchasing, while arrangements for interlibrary loan steadily improve with developments such as the British Library Lending Division in the United Kingdom and the Center for Research Libraries and 'shared cataloging' arrangements in the United States.

Morse has presented data and a model relating to the use of monographs at M.I.T. Science Library.[155] This showed the use in successive years of a sample of titles acquired in one year. Morse found a basic trend of obsolescence, though naturally the actual usage in a year did vary around the expected usage. Fussler and Simon also present a wealth of detail.[80]

It seems likely that, with more research, it will prove possible to develop models for monograph stock policies similar to the models already discussed for serials in this chapter and in Appendix A. One approach would be to divide the monograph holdings into a number of groups by age. Within each age group both the amount and the distribution of demand would be examined. This should shed some light on optimal acquisition policies with respect to current versus retrospective buying and on the relative advantages of discarding various quantities of monographs of different age groups if analyses similar to those just presented for serials were required. However, the results would tend to be in overall terms. They would, for example, indicate what a suitable stock profile with respect to the relative proportions of material in various ages would be if fiscal and spatial pressures necessitated a close matching of stock to demand—as opposed to building comprehensive holdings in specific subject areas. Such models would, then, have some value for the purposes of analysis but in view of variability in demand on individual monographs it is likely, on both theoretical and practical grounds, that individual discarding decisions would best be based on the use of thresholds of demand and judging individual documents by these thresholds regardless of age. This approach will be elaborated in later chapters. However, even if the theoretical analyses are not used for *prescriptive* purposes (to prescribe which documents should be discarded), they should, if soundly based, be usable for *predictive* purposes because they should be able to predict the long-term consequences of using the more practical approach of judging individual documents by criteria of demand and to predict what would constitute a useful stock profile in terms of the age distribution of the stock.

F.   REVIEW

A large number of assumptions have been made during the preceding analyses. Most of them were made for the sake of simplicity. The two fundamental assumptions are that there are two recognisable patterns in the demand for journal literature by workers in any field. More specifically it is assumed that there is an obsolescence effect in individual titles and that the law of diminishing returns operates when the number of journals in a library is increased. These two assumptions appear to be universally accepted in the literature of librarianship, though there has not been unanimity on the precise formulation of either obsolescence or scattering. For present purposes, it is sufficient to demonstrate that these laws have important implications for library planning.

In Section C, the practice of other investigators has been followed in assuming that all titles are to be retained for the same length of time before discarding. This was done because, while it would in fact lead to non-optimal results, it does have the virtue of simplicity and of showing the *manner* in which calculations based on observable patterns of library use can be used to help make policy decisions. This assumption is relaxed in Section D. It may sometimes seem a little unreal in the context of academic libraries to assume that material will be discarded. This is because three considerations impede discarding in practice:

(i) Although the costs of storage are real enough, these costs are not in practice chargeable to the librarian's budget. Therefore, the librarian is motivated to demand more space (which is, in effect, either free or not available) rather than economise on his space requirements. This could be changed if different budgetary procedures were adopted, which made for greater accountability with respect to space costs.

(ii) Current library processing procedures are designed to facilitate the *addition* of books: discarding is generally a finicky and laborious process. If the unit cost of discarding were to rise above a fairly low threshold, it would become more economical *not* to discard but to invest the cost of discarding in a bank, use part of the interest to pay for continued storage and even enjoy the balance of the interest for other purposes and the residual benefit of retaining the books. The decision to discard is, therefore, very sensitive to the relationship between storage costs and discarding costs. The advent of computer-based data processing is likely to reduce dramatically the cost and effort of discarding.

(iii) Although obsolescence is well established as a statistical pattern,* there remains always a possibility that a book discarded today will be needed in the future. If this happens, it could be interpreted as a lack of judgement and, therefore, competence on the part of the

---

*As with scattering, the details are a matter of debate. Browsing in recent volumes of the *Journal of Documentation* provides a convenient introduction.

librarian. A defensive strategy for the librarian is to play safe by avoiding discarding. A relevant consideration here is the substantial improvement in interlibrary loan facilities in recent years—although the burden on large libraries is becoming a source of concern.

Apart from their productivity in terms of the law of scattering, it is assumed that titles do not differ significantly in various other respects: their obsolescence rates, their purchase price, their size and the cost of their binding. This has been done for the sake of simplicity and for ease of calculation. If data indicated that the journals concerned did differ significantly in one or more of these respects, then these variations could easily be incorporated into the calculations; similarly the effects of having different binding policies for different titles could well be explored. But as the assumptions are relaxed, the calculations become more complicated and it may prove more convenient to use this type of analysis to compare various policies than to attempt to compute an optimal solution.

It has also been assumed that the librarians of our imaginary petroleum libraries are model librarians with perfect selection skills who always ensured that the limited number of titles that they did buy were those most in demand. In practice, selection skills are likely to be less than ideal and this will, of course, affect the quality of service. If one hundred titles are acquired and these are not exactly the one hundred titles most in demand, then clearly the actual availability will be less than the ideal achievable with perfect selection skills. In principle, the mismatch between the usefulness of the titles acquired and the usefulness of the ideal selection could be used as a measure of selection performance.* A related consideration is the actual variation in the cost of titles. An average price per title has been assumed throughout for the sake of simplicity. It would be possible to modify the policies to allow for variations in the costs per title. This could very well result in the selection of some less useful titles in lieu of some more useful titles if the latter were substantially more expensive than the former. This could produce a more useful stock for any given expenditure because economising on the expensive title would permit more than one other title in its place.

A major problem in this sort of approach is the difficulty of collecting adequate data, even with sampling techniques. However, with the development of computer-aided data processing of loan records in libraries,

---

*This point was noticed by Cole[61]. It could be reflected in calculations by using a modified scattering coefficient.

full details of all borrowing use become available. Such data inevitably include recorded use but not unrecorded ('in-library') use. However, various investigators have found evidence to suggest that the distribution of 'in-library' use is the same as, or similar to, the distribution of 'recorded' use. McGrath[138] and Pinzelik and Tolliver[176] have shown that in individual libraries the overall 'in-library' use and the 'recorded' use are closely correlated and fluctuate together in a calculable ratio. Fussler and Simon[80] established that this was also true of individual titles, at least in the case of little used material. It seems likely that it is true in all libraries although, of course, the actual ratio will probably vary from library to library and between different types of title within a given library.

The specific ratio of the two kinds of use in different libraries will depend on the manner of provision. For example, at one large Canadian library there is little study space available inside the stacks and the data collection devices of the issue system are at the stack exits. Consequently, out-of-library use is recorded by the computer-based issue system even though the reader merely took the book from the stacks to a reading room and did not remove the book from the library. In contrast, a fully open-access library that does not permit borrowing is likely to be particularly lacking in data on usage.

In Subsections D2 and D3, it was implicitly assumed that success in satisfying demand from stock does not affect the pattern of demand itself. Since physical accessibility is known to be a factor affecting the demand for library services, as Harris[95] and Rosenberg[191,192] have demonstrated, it is likely that even with excellent interlibrary loan facilities, items not in stock will *seem* less accessible to the user. Consequently, users might tend not to request interlibrary loans even though they would have consulted the item had it been in stock and immediately available. Clearly, any administrator would need to be sensitive to this possibility. It is an area in which research is much needed, especially if we make the reasonable assumption that library users adapt their behaviour ('learn') according to their experiences and their consequent expectations of success or frustration.

G. SUMMARY

The first problem to be considered in this book is the optimal size of the library in terms of titles held. The size of a collection is determined by the number of titles acquired and by the length of time they are held. In each case, there is a well-established law of diminishing returns. When examined in conjunction, these laws provide considerable insight into library stock policies. This is illustrated by means of a series of analyses based on the empirical findings of other researchers concerning the use of collections of journals.

Comparable analyses of collections of monographs appear to be possible but so far there is little empirical evidence to use as a basis for developing such analyses.

There are two major difficulties in the practical use of the analyses presented.*

First, there are practical and theoretical difficulties in the collection and analysis of the data required. Automated circulation systems should help, but not until these are conceived and operated as management information systems as well as a record of who has borrowed which title.

Second, the analyses remain incomplete, on present knowledge, because not enough is known about the impact on users of satisfying any given proportion of their demand or about how users react to the satisfying of different proportions of their demand.

Part Two has examined the problem of deciding how much stock a library ought to possess. However, ownership of a document does not mean that a user will be able to find it promptly when he wants it. Part Three is concerned with the problem of assessing how often users fail to find books that the library owns and of identifying factors that cause this failure. Part Four examines two of these factors—binding and borrowing—in some detail.

---

*Nevertheless, a technical library in Preston, England reported changing its holdings on the basis of scattering and obsolescence analyses.[103,104]

Part Three: How Can One Diagnose Faulty Control of Book Availability in a Library?

CHAPTER 3

Diagnosis of Stock Failure

In the previous section, we examined analytical approaches to the problem of determining stock policies with respect to the size of collection. We now examine various techniques for diagnosing stock failure of two kinds:

(a) *Adequacy of stock*: Failure to acquire particular titles that should have been acquired.
(b) *Availability of stock*: Failure to make adequately available the material that has been acquired. It is not sufficient to assume that because a library has purchased a book, this book is available when required by a user.

Subsequently we shall be analysing in depth the most important causes of non-availability of library stocks: loan and duplication policies.

A. STANDARD EXPENDITURE

A simple approach to the adequacy of book provision is to examine expenditure on books and to relate it to the clientele served.[57,139,197] This approach has resulted in British public library circles in reliance on "standards" of library expenditure: that each local authority ought to spend £x per resident on library provision. This is, no doubt, a convenient way of comparing the amount of financial support that libraries are receiving but, as with cooking, expenditure on ingredients does not guarantee the quality of the product. In particular, this approach is quite unhelpful in the management of existing stock.

B.   STANDARD LISTS

An approach that has been extensively used in North America is to select a list of titles judged to be useful to the clientele of a library.[154] This list can be checked against the catalogue to see what proportion is held. This is some test of the quality of selection and of the adequacy of the book fund, but places complete reliance on the assumption that the list used is representative of the users' demands.

A useful extension of this is to test the availability of stock by observing how long it takes to *obtain* a copy of each of the titles from the list that are in the catalogue. The Document Delivery Test developed by Orr and others is a good example of this. The interested reader is strongly recommended to examine both the detailed description by Orr and his co-workers of the Document Delivery Test[171] and also the findings and methodological considerations that were reported after ninety-two medical libraries had been evaluated by it.[172]

C.   DIRECT ASSESSMENT OF READER FRUSTRATION

The abandonment of 'representative' lists in favour of the analysis of the actual searches of library users represents a further refinement. Three examples of this approach will be summarised.

Example No. 1: National Lending Library Survey at Birmingham, 1965

The report of the Committee on Libraries of the British University Grants Committee (the 'Parry Report')[218] contains, in an appendix, a description of a survey conducted at the University of Birmingham Library by staff of the National Lending Library for Science and Technology (now the British Library Lending Division). Users were interviewed as they left the library. Amongst other things, they were asked how many items they had succeeded in finding and how many they had failed to find. This permitted a calculation of the *proportion of searches* that were successful. They were also asked to name the titles that they had failed to find and an immediate search was made by library staff for the elusive items and the actual location noted. Since the location normally implies a cause, this permitted a comparative assessment of the causes of failure, e.g. $x\%$ were out on loan, $y\%$ were being bound, $z\%$ were being catalogued, and so on.

Example No. 2: Lancaster Frustration Survey, 1968

In 1968, the author and his colleagues decided to survey non-availability of stock at the University of Lancaster Library. A secondary objective was to measure the amount of unrecorded use of books inside the library.

Although the National Lending Library survey at Birmingham was taken as the basis of the survey design, two modifications should be noted. Instead of interviewing users as they left, an 'instant diary' was used. This was a brief questionnaire given to users as they arrived and deposited, completed by them (one hopes) as they left. This was expected to be less troublesome to both surveyors and surveyed. The other modification was the incorporation of questions with checkable answers. Users were asked to record the numbers of items *borrowed*, a datum that is also counted at the Library's circulation desk. It was considered that a comparison of the actual circulation as recorded at the circulation desk with the circulation reported on the questionnaires would give some impression of the probable accuracy of the survey.

A questionnaire was designed to extract numerical answers (a copy is reproduced as Fig. 3.1). Since a measure of actual use of the library was intended, a copy was handed to each person entering the library on that day, which had been selected partly because it appeared to be typical. Readers entering the library more than once during the day were asked to record their activities during their second or subsequent visit on a new questionnaire, or alternatively to add further information to their first questionnaire. A count was made of the number of questionnaires handed out and also of the number of visits. At the exit, a box was prominently displayed with a notice asking users to put their completed questionnaires in the box. Every fifteen minutes returned questionnaires were removed from the box and a note was made of all titles noted in response to Question 6 ('Please list the author, title and classmark, if known, of the long loan books, journals, etc. that you were not able to borrow or consult'). As quickly as possible the exact physical location of these items was ascertained. Although it had not seemed possible to establish the location of items *at the actual time that they could not be found*, the method adopted did establish the location within a few minutes of the readers leaving the library.

UNIVERSITY OF LANCASTER

LIBRARY SURVEY

Last year the University Library began a Government-sponsored research project on the efficient management of library services. This questionnaire is being given out because we need some information which we cannot collect in any other way. Please cooperate by answering the questions carefully and so HELP THE LIBRARY TO HELP YOU. Accurate information will be very useful to us in trying to make our service better for you.

QUESTIONNAIRE

It is ESSENTIAL to give NUMERICAL answers relating ONLY to THIS VISIT to the Library, however untypical of your normal behaviour it may be.

1. How many books, journals, etc. did you bring with you to use in the library on this visit?

SHORT LOAN BOOKS

2. How many Short Loan books did you borrow on this visit?

3. How many Short Loan books which you wished to borrow were you not able to obtain on this visit?

Please list the author, title and classmark, if known, of the Short Loan books which you were not able to borrow:

Author	Title	Classmark (if known)
1.		
2.		
3.		
4.		
5.		
6.		

LONG LOAN BOOKS, JOURNALS etc.

4. How many long loan books, journals, etc. did you borrow on this visit?
[N.B. "Borrowed", in this context, means "issued at the service desk, normally for use outside the Library."]

5. How many long loan or 'reference only' books, journals, etc. did you consult during this visit but not borrow?

[N.B. "Consult", in this context means "use within the Library", but please include any photocopies you asked to have made.]

6. How many long loan books, journals, etc. did you wish to borrow or consult, but were NOT able to obtain during this visit?

Please list the author, title and classmark, if known, of the long loan books, journals, etc. that you were not able to borrow or consult:

	Author	Title	Classmark (if known)
1.			
2.			
3.			
4.			
5.			
6.			
7.			
8.			
9.			
10.			

7. What is your status? (Please tick the appropriate box)

1. Undergraduate 1st year   4. Postgraduate

2. Undergraduate 2nd year   5. Member of academic staff

3. Undergraduate 3rd year   6. Other: please specify

8. Please state:

If UNDERGRADUATE: Major or intended major: ------------------------------

If POSTGRADUATE: Department -------------------- Degree sought -------

If ACADEMIC STAFF: Department ---

Thank you for your cooperation.
A. G. Mackenzie
Librarian

PLEASE PUT THE COMPLETED QUESTIONNAIRE IN THE BOX PROVIDED AS YOU LEAVE

Fig. 3.1. Questionnaire of Lancaster Frustration Survey, 1967.

(i) Questionnaires handed out   789
     Questionnaires returned   563
     Percentage returned: 71%
(ii) Short Loan issue (actual)   304
     Short Loan issue (questionnaire)   193
     Percentage recorded: 63%
(iii) Long Loan issue (actual)   188
     Long Loan issue (questionnaire)   107
     Percentage recorded: 57%

The three percentages 71, 63 and 57 are in close enough agreement to suggest that the returned questionnaires presented a balanced picture.

Failure to Find Items

The main purpose of the survey had been to assess the relative importance of the factors that prevent readers from finding the material that they want. 165 Long Loan items were recorded as not available in response to Question 6: of these 165 items, 33 were unidentifiable from the information recorded; the remaining 132 fall into the following categories:

	Frequency	Titles
1. On loan	39	38
2. On shelves	23	18
3. In use	11	8
4. On Short Loan shelves	10	10
5. Missing	9	9
6. Not owned or on order	9	8
7. At binding	6	6
8. On loan but also on Short Loan shelves	6	6
9. On loan but also Short Loan copy on loan	4	3
10. On loan but also available in stock		
11. Missing but replacement on order	3	1
12. On order: not yet arrived	2	2
13. Missing but another copy available in stock		
14. Awaiting photocopying	1	1
15. Awaiting reshelving	1	1
16. On loan, another copy at binding	1	1 .
17. Kept at service desk	1	1
18. Exhibit removed during survey	1	1
Total	132	117

A curious feature of those results is category 2, the second largest category, in which 23 items were in the correct place on the shelves when checked; similarly a number of items sought on the open shelves had been transferred to the closed access reserve collection, where they were available at the time of search. These two facts suggest poor searching, or possibly inadequate or misleading guiding of the library.

Example No. 3: Cambridge Failure Analysis, 1969–1970[221]

During 1969 and 1970 the staff of the Library Management Research Unit at Cambridge University Library developed another approach to this problem. Readers were asked to complete a slip of paper each time they failed to find a book and place it where they thought it should be. As library staff replace books, a note of where the book has been can be matched with slip placed by the reader. The probability that a user will in fact complete a slip can be assessed independently by interviewing a sample of users as they leave the library.

D.   CONCLUSIONS

Comparison of expenditure per head of population served may help identify libraries that deserve closer examination but does little more.

The checking of lists against catalogues is a very convenient method of testing the adequacy of a library's stock, but depends entirely on the acceptance of the assumption that it is representative of users' demands. Seeking some or all of the actual documents as in the Document Delivery Test is a more meaningful test of availability because it involves an objective test of the library's performance in making documents available. Even so, the researcher—probably a professional librarian—is likely to be unusually skilled at finding the books in a complex open-access library.

It is much more satisfactory to monitor reader failure *directly* because the titles sought *are* representative and the failures that may stem from inadequate user know-how are real and, on the Lancaster evidence, important factors in the failure of the library service to bring book and reader together. However, since a user considers that the library is unlikely to hold a given item, then he may not bother to seek it in the library. Consequently, failure caused by the collection being inadequate or irrelevant is likely to be underestimated. Nevertheless, the direct assessment of reader frustration is a practical and important step towards responsible library management and if the data collected are used to improve book availability, it is likely that readers will, through increased confidence, try to use the library for a fuller range of their needs.

The next step is to examine specific causes of failure in some detail. Such an examination may lead to changes in procedure or policy, which can reduce the amount of reader frustration in a relatively cost-effective manner. Part Four is devoted to the examination of two such causes of failure. In the next chapter, binding arrangements are considered and then there is a detailed examination of the important and complex problem of the frustration caused by permitting users to borrow books.

Part Four: How Can Book Availability
in a Library be Improved?

CHAPTER 4

Binding Arrangements

The previous chapter described how books owned by a library are not necessarily available when sought. Techniques for assessing the relative importance of various causes of 'stock failure' were discussed. Although most books bought for libraries are already bound when acquired, some categories are normally bound *after* acquisition. This binding necessarily involves an absence from the shelves. The problem is to weigh the benefits of greater availability against the costs of achieving it.

(i) Periodicals that are received in parts (e.g. monthly, quarterly, weekly) are normally sent for binding when all the parts that constitute a 'volume' have been received. This typically involves an absence from the shelves some 3–18 months after acquisition.

(ii) Some books are published only in paperback form and these are usually bound to protect them from the wear and tear of library use. Such books may be rebound or strengthened before delivery, but, more commonly—especially in academic libraries—these books will be received in paperback form and then sent to the binders before they are made accessible to readers by being placed on the library's shelves. This absence occurs when the books are new—a period during which demand is likely to be relatively high.

(iii) Bound books that have been subjected to unusually heavy usage may need rebinding. In strict bibliographical terminology, a 'book' is a printed text: the binding (in whatever form) is not a part of the book but a protective container. Modern books when issued by the publisher in 'bound' or 'hard-back' form are not usually bound, in the strict sense, but 'cased'. Casing lends itself much more readily to mechanised production but the hinges that attach the boards to the book are much weaker than in a properly taped and sewn binding. Consequently, a cased book is less strong and falls apart sooner than a properly bound one. This is particularly common with popular textbooks and novels.

The absence of books from the shelves whilst at the binders can be expected to cause frustration when readers seek the items concerned. The length of these absences and the inconvenience they cause constitute a frequent source of complaint in academic libraries.

One response to these problems is for the library to have its own domestic bindery on the library premises. Such a bindery could be expected to reduce frustration by involving a briefer absence from the shelves.* Furthermore, even when desired items are in the bindery, they can normally be promptly fetched.

Against this, a domestic bindery is certain to lack the volume of business that permits commercial binders (with hundreds of employees) to achieve economies of scale.

In brief, a domestic bindery is likely to have higher unit costs but may result in a better library service from the user's point of view. An attempt to explore the play-off between cost and benefit was made in Chapter 2, Subsection C3. However, when it was urgently necessary to explore this problem in the University of Lancaster Library in the summer of 1968, there was no readily available data on obsolescence or scattering in its multidisciplinary collection and a more direct approach was followed. The numerical data should be treated cautiously because the circumstances permitted very little data-gathering. Nevertheless, the details are presented because the cost-benefit analysis adopted represents an original and valid approach to a problem that is relevant to all medium and large libraries.

The workload was then assessed as 6,000 volumes to be sent to commercial binderies at an average cost of £1·15 per volume. A number of other British university libraries that had domestic binderies were asked for detailed information, but relevant details were often not available. In the light of the replies, it was decided to assume a unit cost of £1·20 per volume for domestic binding (£0·05 higher than with a commercial bindery) and a mean delay of 4 weeks instead of 10.

Against this increased cost, a domestic bindery could be expected to offer the following benefits:

---

*This chapter was based on British experience. Since commercial binderies in the United States appear to offer a substantially faster service (e.g. 3 or 4 weeks), the calculations in this chapter might work out somewhat differently for a library in the United States.

(a) A reduction in clerical and professional labour in the preparation of books for despatch to the bindery (fewer records, no packing, etc.).

(b) A reduction in users' frustration on account of faster binding.

(c) A reduction in the number and, therefore, total cost of interlibrary loans in cases where material is urgently required. With a domestic bindery, such material can simply be fetched.

These three are difficult to assess in monetary terms. Nevertheless, progress can be made.

The Frustration Survey described in the previous chapter showed that on one day at the main library alone, 6 items then at binding were wanted. This survey had about a two-thirds response, so we can expect the actual number of such items to have been 9: in a full year, allowing for seasonal fluctuations, the total number is unlikely to have been less than 1,200. Clearly, data derived from a series of Frustration Surveys would have been much more satisfactory, but it was not practical to collect additional data at that time. Even if the domestic bindery's turn-round time is as high as 4 weeks instead of 10 weeks, this number would be cut by 60% or 720; the remaining 480 items are on the premises and could therefore be made available quite promptly if they were requested. If only half of the frustrated readers asked for material being bound, then a further 240 requests would be satisfied. This makes a total of 960, but in a domestic bindery it would be possible to allocate selective priorities to heavily used titles, thus cutting their 'down-time' and increasing the figure of 960.

As regards interlibrary loans to meet unsatisfied requests, little information was available, but the cost of these could perhaps add up to £100 a year. Bindery equipment costs were taken as £5,000, to be written off over 10 years—namely £500 per annum.

The annual costs can be summarised as follows.

	Domestic		Commercial	
6,000 volumes bound	at £1·20	£7,200	at £1·15	£6,900
Depreciation on capital		£ 500		—
Additional interlibrary loan expenses		—		£ 100
		£7,700		£7,000

This suggests a difference in known costs of £700. In this case, the University Grants Committee ruled that the bindery equipment could be included in the grant to furnish the extension to the library so the cost to the university became zero and the difference in operating costs became only £200.

For the price of £200, the library expected to reap the following advantages:

1. An additional 1,000 or more frustrated requests would be satisfied (at a mean cost of £0·20 each).
2. An expected reduction in staff time and fewer records in the library ((a) above).
3. The period of waiting for documents to return from binding would be significantly reduced.

Comment

Domestic binderies are normally justified on the grounds of their intangible benefits rather than their cheaper costs; on the other hand, present methods of financing the university result in a part of the cost not being charged to the library concerned. This rather crude cost-benefit approach seemed to clarify the issues involved and a domestic bindery became operational early in 1971.

In any replication of this approach, it would be desirable to use more sophisticated approaches to the quantification that the urgency of this particular study did not permit.

1. The presumed unit costs of a domestic bindery were based on rather vague information from other libraries.
2. It would be more appropriate to handle the capital investment in binding equipment by means of discounted cash flow techniques rather than depreciation.
3. Very little data were available upon which to base the estimate of the amount of frustration being caused by binding delays at Lancaster.

These weaknesses are valid criticisms of the actual study itself but they do not invalidate the *approach* used since more reliable data could be collected given time and resources. The basic approach was to assess two alternative strategies in terms of cost and benefit. The decision would have been simpler if either the cost or the benefit had been the same for both policies; for example if one binding policy had involved a lower level of frustration for the same cost—or if, for the same level of frustration, one binding policy had cost less. In the event, both costs and frustration levels were different and it was essentially an informed value judgement that it would be worthwhile to reduce frustration at the price of increased binding costs. This illustrates well, in a library context, the basic nature of cost-benefit analysis. In fact, the approach adopted does much more than this because the measure of service adopted—immediate availability on the shelf when sought—is the *same measure* as has been adopted, elsewhere in this book in the context of stock control decisions. Should the librarian invest in additional titles?—in continued storage?—in duplicate copies?—in the inconvenience of shorter loan periods?—in a domestic bindery? Insofar as these can be related to a common measure of service and a common measure of cost, it is possible not only to adopt a cost-benefit approach to each decision problem separately, but, *much more significantly, to compare the relative benefits of increased investment in one compared with another.* For example, how far would the librarian improve the standard of service by investing in a domestic bindery at the expense of the number of titles acquired? A basis of this kind is essential for meaningful progress towards determining the optimal deployment of a library's budget.

In the rest of this part, Chapters 5–9 examine a comparable approach towards another aspect of library stock control: the complex relationships involved in relating loan and duplication policies to the reduction of user frustration.

CHAPTER 5

Loan and Duplication Problems: Individual Titles

In the previous chapter, we examined binding as a cause of 'stock failure'. A more important and more complex problem is the stock failure caused by allowing users to borrow books. Every library has a loan policy of some kind, even if it is that no books may be removed from the library. University libraries commonly have several policies: some material may be confined to the library; some may be borrowable from a reserve collection for a few hours; the rest is usually borrowable for a longer period—the length of time permitted often depending on the status of the borrower. Furthermore, there are also wide variations from library to library in terms of length of loan period, renewal policies, fine rates, and the administration of overdues.

A. THE BASIC RELATIONSHIP

This variety seems to stem from complex conflicts of interest and it is necessary to try to analyse the structure of the problem.

1. For the individual borrower, a long loan period is desirable because it gives him greater freedom to retain a book at leisure without being bothered by overdue correspondence, fines and the need to bring it back. Another borrower might ask the library to recall this book, but this may not happen very often. He is, of course, quite free to return the book early—as soon as he has finished with it—but a long loan period is definitely more convenient for the individual borrower.

2. For everybody else, this borrower's lengthy loan period is *inconvenient* because there is always some probability that someone else may

want that particular book. The longer the borrower retains it, the longer it is absent from the shelf and the less chance anyone else has of finding it immediately when they want it. For everyone, except the borrower, a *shorter* loan period is more convenient. The fact that every library user plays both the role of borrower and the role of 'everybody else' does not remove this conflict of interest.

Now although books can be made more readily available by inducing borrowers to retain them for relatively short periods only, five further complications arise:

3. The level of demand varies enormously from book to book or, to put it another way, the probability that a book will be sought whilst it is out on loan varies greatly. There is little justification for curtailing the loan of material that is unlikely to be asked for, but for material known to be in heavy demand there is a very good case for wanting borrowers to return their books quickly if the frustration of other would-be borrowers is to be minimised. It does not make the librarian's task any easier that the probability that another reader will seek a book is not easy to assess.

4. Inducing the borrower to return a book soon is not the only way of reducing the frustration of other would-be borrowers because one can always provide another copy. Duplication is clearly an acceptable alternative strategy. However, it must be noted that although shorter loan periods and additional copies both increase the chances that a copy will be on the shelf, these policies differ in two important respects. First, shorter loan periods are definitely less convenient for the individual borrower, and to this extent undesirable. Second, the provision of duplicate copies uses up money and labour that the library could well have used for other purposes—such as another, *different* title. To this extent, duplication is also undesirable. The policy of providing different titles as deliberate alternatives in the event of failure to find the book originally sought is difficult to assess because little seems to be known about the 'substitutability' of titles.

5. If a book is not on the shelf, then it can still be made available by means of a reservation and, if appropriate, by recalling it from the reader who has it. To the extent to which this is an acceptable substitute for immediate availability on the shelf, this arrangement reduces the importance of 'immediate availability' and thereby permits longer loan periods and less duplication. Acceptability apart, this cumbersome procedure of reservation and recall is clearly unsuitable for those who are not seeking a specific title but are browsing, perhaps purposefully, for inspiration or amusement. If such a reader is browsing along the shelves, then it is

clearly important that appropriate material should be on the shelves. Otherwise, unless he also browses in the catalogues, the reader will remain unaware of the existence of suitable material and the provision of procedures for reservation and recall will be irrelevant.

6. Administrative aspects must also be considered since not all loan and duplication policies are equally easy to administer.

7. Similarly, it is essential to consider political aspects. It is not enough to devise loan and duplication policies: they have to be acceptable to the public served. In libraries, as in other public services, the users are, indirectly, the policy makers. It can be argued quite plausibly that the widespread practice of allowing more liberal loan privileges to faculty than to undergraduates stems more from the power structure of universities than from any attempt by librarians to manage their resources affectively.

It will be quite clear from these observations that the wide variations in loan and duplication policies reflect quite complicated relationships involving a number of conflicting objectives. Any rational loan and duplication policy must be a considered compromise.

In order to clarify the roles of the various factors, a convenient strategy is to relate each factor to the chances that a copy will be on the shelves when a book is sought. This has been called 'immediate availability'.* Apart from the number of copies held, the two critical factors determining the immediate availability of any given book are:

—the frequency with which the book is sought (its 'popularity'); and,
—the length of time it is off the shelf when used.

The basic relationship is in the following form:

(i) *For any given loan period*, the chances of a copy being on the shelves when sought varies inversely with the popularity. The greater the popularity, the lower the immediate availability; the less the popularity, the higher the immediate availability. (See Diagram 5.1.)

*It is necessary to distinguish between:
(i) The probability that a given book will be available when sought.
(ii) The probability that users will find the books they seek.
In this book, the term 'immediate availability' is used to denote (i), and 'satisfaction level' is used to denote (ii), which is the weighted mean 'immediate availability' of a collection of many books, weighted by the distribution of demand, as is explained in Chapter 7. This seems better than using 'satisfaction level' for both (i) and (ii) and relying on the context to prevent confusion, as in Buckland[46,50] and Buckland et al.[52]

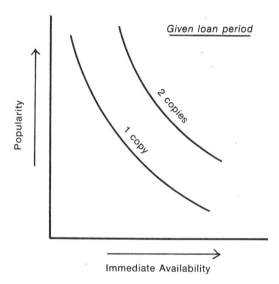

Given loan period

Popularity

2 copies

1 copy

Immediate Availability

Diagram 5.1.   The relationship between popularity and immediate availability for any given loan period. (This diagram illustrates the inverse relationship. The precise shape of the curves will vary according to the details of the individual situation.)

(ii) *For any given popularity*, the length of the loan period and the immediate availability are inversely related. The longer the loan period, the lower the immediate availability; the shorter the loan period, the higher the immediate availability. (See Diagram 5.2.)

(iii) *For any given level of immediate availability*, the popularity and the length of the loan period are necessarily also inversely related. The greater the popularity, the shorter the loan period has to be; the less the popularity, the longer the loan period can be. (See Diagram 5.3.)

(iv) *Duplication.* Increasing the number of copies available, like shortening the length of loan periods, increases immediate availability. To this extent, it is an alternative strategy. The relationship can be seen in Diagrams 5.1, 5.2 and 5.3 by comparing the curve for one copy with the curve for two copies.

These relationships have been described in some detail because they lead to a most significant conclusion. If the library is intended to make documents available and if promptness is a virtue, then *the cardinal rule of library stock control is that both the loan period and the duplication*

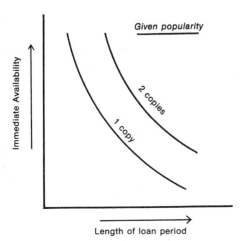

Diagram 5.2.   The relationship between immediate availability and length of loan period for any given popularity. (This diagram illustrates the inverse relationship. The precise shape of the curves will vary according to the details of the individual situation.)

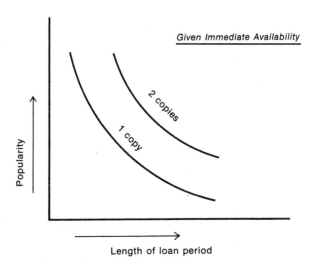

Diagram 5.3.   Relationship between popularity and length of loan period for any given immediate availability. (This diagram illustrates the inverse relationship. The precise shape of the curves will vary according to the details of the individual situation.)

policy should be related to the level of demand for the title and to each other. In the next two sections, we explore two alternative approaches to quantifying the *a priori* relationships we have just described. The advantage of quantification is that it adds proportion and precision to relationships that have been perceived in a rather subjective manner.

B. MEASUREMENT: ANALYTICAL APPROACHES

B1. Lancaster Short Loan Collection

During 1967 an attempt was made to use an analytical approach to aid day-to-day duplication decisions in a reserve collection at the University of Lancaster Library. This collection is known as the Short Loan collection and contains items expected to be in heavy demand. Books are removed from the open shelves and are kept behind a service desk.

In general, the teaching staff are relied upon to give prior notice of books that are likely to be heavily used, and of the appropriate number of copies of each, since it is they who direct the student's reading. Nevertheless, the library staff considered that both choice of titles and number of copies ought to be improved.

A list is displayed and would-be borrowers ask for the book they want. They are only allowed one book at a time and, if it is available, it is lent to them for a few hours at a time. There is a system of twenty-two fixed loan periods as follows:

Book borrowed	is due back by
Monday–Friday	
Before 12.30	13.00
12.30–16.30	17.00
16.30–21.00	21.30
After 21.00	10.00 next morning
Saturday	
Before 12.30	13.00
After 12.30	10.00 next Monday

This pattern of morning, afternoon, evening and overnight borrowing appears to fit the daily rhythm of the university fairly well. The loan regulations are enforced with heavy fines—then £0·05 for the first fifteen minutes, £0·10 per hour for up to four hours and £0·05 per hour after that.

A loan may be renewed unless another reader has reserved it. In general features, if not in detail, it is similar to other reserve collections that have long been common in North America and that are rapidly becoming so in the United Kingdom. The importance of the Short Loan collection in undergraduate library use is considerable.

In 1970–1971 when there were less than 3,000 full-time students at the university, no less than 78,235 loans were made from the Short Loan collection of the main library at Bailrigg, where most of the university was sited.

The first problem was to define in a measurable form a suitable standard of service. One simple expedient would have been to observe how many of the books were available at any given time. This was rejected because it takes no account of the variation in demand from book to book, and as a standard of service it was clearly unsatisfactory because the proportion available could be increased by adding to the collection books that were *not* in demand. If the standard of service adopted was to be relevant to the users needs, then it would have to be related, more or less directly, to the demand expressed by the users. We decided that it would be reasonable to observe how often a copy of a book was available at the time it was requested. We defined this measure as 'immediate availability'. The 'immediate availability' of a book was the proportion of times it was immediately available when requested. This can conveniently be expressed as a percentage thus:

$$\% \text{ immediate availability} = \frac{100 \times \text{No. of requests immediately satisfied}}{\text{Total no. of requests}}.$$

This concept is admittedly a somewhat crude measure of the standard of service; for example, it does not take fully into account the fact that requests that are not immediately satisfied can almost invariably be satisfied on some later occasion if the user has sufficient time and persistence. However, such delays are *prima facie* undesirable, and in the circumstances immediate availability seemed to us to be a reasonable measure of the standard of service. Accordingly, throughout this section the terms 'available' and 'satisfied' are used to mean *immediately* available and *immediately* satisfied.

The four key factors appeared to be:

(i) the number of requests,
(ii) the loan period,
(iii) the number of copies, and
(iv) immediate availability.

It is, in fact, convenient to combine the first two of these factors: if the number of requests occurring during any given span of time is divided by the number of loan periods in the same span of time, then we have an 'average request rate per loan period'. The effect on the average request rate per loan period of an increase or decrease in the number of requests will be clear. So too is the effect of a change in the loan period: to lengthen the loan period is to reduce the number of loan periods in any given span of time, and so the average request rate per loan period is increased; conversely, the shortening of the loan period decreases the average request rate per loan period. Although the concept of an average request rate is used throughout this section, it should not be forgotten that the effect of a change in the length of the loan period can readily be assessed by calculating a new request rate.

In investigating the request pattern, we assume initially that there is an ascertainable average request rate for a given title, and that the Poisson distribution* can adequately describe the variations in the observed numbers of requests in individual loan periods.

In order to establish the availability rate we need to know both the number of satisfied requests and the total number of requests. If the number of requests for a title in one loan period is equal to, or less than, the number of copies available, then all requests will be satisfied immediately. If the number of requests exceeds the number of copies, and if, as we assume, a copy cannot be borrowed more than once within a single loan period, then the number of satisfied requests cannot exceed the number of copies.

We define n as the number of copies of a given title and s as the number of requests for it in any single loan period so that when $0 \leqslant s \leqslant n$, then s requests are satisfied and when $s > n$, then n requests are satisfied. Since $P(s)$ expresses the relative frequency of s requests being made in a loan period

$$\text{Percentage immediate availability} = \frac{100\left[\sum_{s=0}^{n} sP(s) + \sum_{s=n+1}^{\infty} nP(s)\right]}{\sum_{s=0}^{\infty} sP(s)}.$$

We now have a relationship involving:

---

*The Poisson distribution is a mathematical formula widely used by statisticians to simulate the occurrence of events that appear to occur at random, i.e. following no known pattern. Details may be found in most textbooks on statistics.

(i) the number of requests,
(ii) the loan period,
(iii) the number of copies, and
(iv) percentage immediate availability.

From this we can calculate the dependence of the availability rate on such factors as

(a) the length of the loan period, and
(b) the number of copies in stock.

In the case of the Short Loan collection, a reduction in the length of loan period has been considered undesirable, and our attention has, therefore, been focused on predicting the correct number of copies. This information is reproduced as Table 5.1.

Table 5.1. Percentage Immediate Availability in Relation to the Request Rate and the Number of Copies Provided.*

Requests per day	Copies provided									Copies required for		
	1	2	3	4	5	6	7	8	9	80%	90%	95%
0·4	95	100								1	1	1
0·5	94	100								1	1	2
0·6	93	100								1	1	2
0·7	92	100								1	1	2
0·8	91	99	100							1	1	2
0·9	90	99	100							1	1	2
1	88	99	100							1	2	2
2	79	97	100							2	2	2
3	70	93	99	100						2	2	3
4	63	90	98	100						2	2	3
5	57	86	96	99	100					2	3	3
6	52	81	94	98	100					2	3	4
7	47	77	92	97	99	100				3	3	4
8	43	73	89	96	99	100				3	4	4
9	40	69	86	95	98	99	100			3	4	4
10	37	65	83	93	98	99	100			3	4	5
12	32	58	78	89	96	98	99	100		4	5	5
14	28	52	72	85	93	97	99	100		4	5	6
16	25	47	66	80	90	95	98	99	100	4	5	6
18	22	43	61	76	86	93	97	98	99	5	6	7
20	20	39	57	71	82	90	95	98	99	5	6	7

*In this table the request rate is given on a per day basis (four loan periods per day) instead of per loan period. The numbers have been rounded.

The results in Table 5.1 were based on the hypothesis that the pattern of requests predicted by the Poisson distribution would not differ significantly from the actual pattern of requests in the collection concerned. The ideal situation for testing this hypothesis would be where it was feasible to record *all* requests (not only satisfied requests) without the user's knowledge, and where the user could not tell in advance whether or not an item was available. The Short Loan collection within the University of Lancaster Library corresponds closely to this ideal situation; consequently, for a period of two weeks during May 1967 all requests were examined. Satisfied requests were already being recorded on the date labels in each item: the date stamped recorded the day of issue, and its position on the data label the loan period within that day. Arrangements were made for the library staff to note briefly on a piece of paper the details of each request that was not immediately satisfied. Users are unlikely to have known in advance whether or not an item would be available, since it is not normally possible for them to see if there is still a copy of a desired item on the shelves; however, we cannot rule out the possibility that one user may occasionally have learned from another that all copies were already on loan. To the best of our knowledge, none of the users was aware that data concerning their requests was being collected.

During these two weeks 2,010 requests were recorded, and the immediate availability rate for the collection as a whole was established as 90%.

A small random sample of 24 titles was taken from the collected data and the distribution of request frequency examined. Some patterns emerged more than once. For example, more than one title had been used once in one loan period and not at all in the remaining 43 loan periods. Thirteen different patterns of use emerged: in each case the total number of requests occurring during the fortnight was divided by the number of loan periods during the survey (44) in order to produce an average request rate per loan period for each title. The Poisson distribution was then used to predict an expected pattern of requests for each average request rate. The observed and the expected (Poisson) frequencies are tabulated in Table 5.2. A statistical analysis (the 'Chi-squared' test) was applied to see whether the differences between the observed and expected frequencies were greater than could be accounted for by chance. In 12 out of 13 cases there no such differences at the 90% level of significance. In view of this similarity, the use of the Poisson distribution for this purpose appears to be justified.

We have demonstrated how a simple table could be produced to show

Table 5.2. Comparison of Patterns of Observed and Expected Requests.

R	O	E	O	E	O	E	O	E	O	E
0	15	14·12	23	24·37	26	28·57	29	29·90	35	33·50
1	13	16·05	16	14·40	17	12·34	13	11·55	7	9·14
2	11	9·12	5	4·25	1	2·66	2	2·23	1	1·25
3	5	3·45	0	0·84	0	0·38	0	0·29	1	0·11
4	0	0·98	0	0·12	0	0·04	0	0·03	0	0·008
5	0	0·22	0	0·01	—	—	—	—	—	—
6	0	0·04	—	—	—	—	—	—	—	—
7	0	0·007	—	—	—	—	—	—	—	—
	Chi-sq.: 2·967		Chi-sq.: 1·362		Chi-sq.: 3·457		Chi-sq.: 0·548		Chi-sq.: 7·566	
	DF: 7		DF: 5		DF: 4		DF: 4		DF: 4	
0	31	32·74	33	32·74	34	35·05	40	40·18	37	35·86
1	13	9·67	9	9·67	10	7·97	4	3·65	5	7·34
2	0	1·43	2	1·43	0	0·90	0	0·17	2	0·75
3	0	0·14	0	0·14	0	0·07	0	0·005	0	0·05
4	0	0·01	0	0·01	—	—	—	—	—	—
	Chi-sq.: 2·816		Chi-sq.: 0·428		Chi-sq.: 1·524		Chi-sq.: 0·205		Chi-sq.: 2·913	
	DF: 4		DF: 4		DF: 3		DF: 3		DF: 3	
0	43	43·01	42	42·04	42	41·10	R = No. of requests			
1	1	0·98	2	1·91	1	2·80	O = Observed frequency			
2	0	0·01	0	0·04	1	0·10	E = Frequency predicted			
	Chi-sq.: 0·012		Chi-sq.: 0·048		Chi-sq.: 9·742		by the Poisson			
	DF: 2		DF: 2		DF: 2		distribution			

90% Significance thresholds:

7DF	5DF	4DF	3DF	2DF
12·02	9·24	7·78	6·25	4·60

Note that some of the expected frequencies in Table 5.1 are < 5. Recommended practice is that cells should be combined to ensure that expected frequencies ⩾ 5. However, the data are such that this would have eliminated most of the cells and seriously reduced the scope for testing. Although the use of cells with expected values < 5 means that the Chi-squared values are approximations, it should be remembered that we have no less than 13 independent tests. Furthermore, the Chi-squared values are in fact very low, implying a close match in most cases.

the minimum number of copies required for different levels of availability and for various average request rates. If it is known in advance what the average request rate will be, then it is a very simple matter to discover how many copies will be needed to maintain any desired level of availability. Unfortunately, it may not be easy to predict the average request rate for any given title.

The information that could normally be made available to the librarian is the number of students who have been advised to read an item and the span of time during which they are all expected to read it (e.g. the date by which an essay should be completed). If b students request an item once only during a period of time containing p loan periods, then the request rate can be written

$$r = \frac{b}{p}.$$

It would be rash, however, to assume that each item will in fact be requested once and once only by each student. Some may not request it at all because they have access to another copy elsewhere, or because they simply do not bother. Others may make more than one request because one borrowing was insufficient or because the book was not available when first requested. These conflicting tendencies might cancel each other out but it may be better to assume that

$$r = x \cdot \frac{b}{p},$$

where x is a quantity, a parameter, which corresponds to this variation in user behaviour. Further investigation might reveal that the value of x tended to remain constant for a particular group of students, or for a particular course, or even for a particular title—but such an investigation would be laborious. In any case, the people most closely concerned—the Service Desk staff and the teaching staff—should be able to estimate from their experience the number of requests for each item.

The main difficulty in the use of this approach for planning for future demand lies in predicting the average request rate. It is necessary, therefore, to explore the consequences of inaccurate prediction.

For example, if the average request rate is expected to be between 0·5 and 1·3 requests per loan period, then we can examine the likely consequences of different decisions about the number of copies to be provided. (See Table 5.3.)

Similarly, if the request rate could only be established as lying between two and four per loan period, then at least we should have the information in Table 5.4.

At the collection actually studied, it happened to be easy to record unsatisfied requests once it had been decided to do so. Nevertheless, the situation might well arise, at Lancaster or elsewhere, in which data on unsatisfied requests was needed retrospectively for a period during which

Table 5.3.

Average request rate	% immediate availability resulting from the provision of			
	1	2	3	4 copies
	(%)	(%)	(%)	(%)
0·5	78·7	96·7	99·6	99·96
1·5	51·8	81·3	94·0	98·4

Table 5.4.

Average request rate	% immediate availability resulting from the provision of			
	3	4	5	6 copies
	(%)	(%)	(%)	(%)
2	89·1	96·2	98·9	99·7
4	66·3	80·5	89·7	95·1

it had not been collected; in different circumstances it may not be practicable to record the number of unsatisfied requests at all. In such cases, it is necessary to rely on an estimate based on the number of satisfied requests (i.e. loans). A technical note on doing this may be found in Appendix B.

Summary

The examination of the Short Loan collection at the University of Lancaster began with two aims:

—How well was it working?
—How far could a quantitative approach be helpful in taking routine decisions about the number of copies to be provided?

When it was realised that the unsatisfied requests could conveniently be recorded, the immediate availability rate was determined and discovered to be somewhat higher than had been expected.

A mathematical relationship between the factors concerned can indeed be established. The results displayed in Table 5.1 illustrate the most important aspect of duplication: *that the marginal benefit of adding an extra copy falls off steadily as the level of immediate availability rises.*

Conversely, as the level of immediate availability rises, so the cost of achieving an extra 5% immediate availability also rises. Doubling the number of copies will not double the immediate availability. The main impediment to the easy use of this table lies in the difficulty in predicting the level of demand.*

B2. Mathematical Theory of Queues

It would seem a logical development of the previous section to apply the mathematical theory of queues† to loan and duplication problems—not just in the relatively straightforward context of a reserve collection, but of the general collection on the open shelves. After the completion of the work in the previous section, P. M. Morse's book *Library effectiveness: a systems approach* [155] was published. Much of this book is concerned with the application of the mathematical theory of queues to book availability. Morse is not concerned with a reserve collection but with the general collections at M.I.T. Science Library. Careful exposition is given of the way in which these models can be related to borrowing, duplication and availability. This is done in some detail using, for the most part, the technical terminology of queuing theory.

There may be no doubt that book availability is basically a 'queuing problem'. Also, there may be no doubt that models based on the mathematical theory of queues can be used to give considerable insight into the relationships between the various factors.

If, on the other hand, it is desired to go beyond basic insights and especially if it is desired to model an actual library in detail, then the mathematical theory of queues suffers from serious limitations.

(i) It is based on the assumption that requests for a given book occur at random with an ascertainable mean request rate and that this process can be validly represented by the Poisson distribution.‡ Neither Morse nor any other researcher has produced evidence that this is a justifiable assumption for a collection other than a closed access reserve collection.

*For further reading on reserve collections, Simmons[202] is strongly recommended.

†The mathematical theory of queues comprises a suite of mathematical models more sophisticated than the analyses presented in the preceding section, which are used to analyse the probable consequences of making changes in situations in which queues occur, such as toll gates, check-out counters, etc. For details, see Morse[155] or textbooks on operations research.

‡Llinas and O'Neill[134] have recently demonstrated that this assumption does affect the results significantly. They computed the differences in terms of book availability between requests arriving 'at random' and requests arriving in a cyclic pattern.

(ii) It is based on the assumption that borrowers return books at random with an ascertainable mean retention period and that this can be represented by a negative exponential distribution. Morse adduces no data in support of this assumption. In the next section, it will be shown that a quite different distribution consistently emerges.

(iii) Some features of the borrowing process do not appear to be amenable to treatment by the mathematical theory of queues—notably the prevalence of 'mixed' loan periods (e.g. two weeks for undergraduates; four weeks for staff); the tendency for only *some* would-be borrowers to make a reservation if a book is not immediately available; and the special problem of in-library use in relation to borrowing.

(iv) Except in the simplest circumstances, the equations rapidly become rather intractable and difficult to handle.

These considerations lead to the conclusion that in most circumstances the mathematical theory of queues is unsuitable for the study of book availability in libraries except for the exploration of basic relationships and rough approximations.

C. MEASUREMENT: EMPIRICAL SIMULATION

After the Short Loan collection at Lancaster had been examined by means of an analytical approach, attention was focused on the much more complex and important problem of loan and duplication policies for the general collection on the open shelves. For this a quite different approach was used for the detailed determination of the relationships between loan period, duplication and immediate availability.

The vast majority of the books are kept on the open shelves and this involves three major complications:

(i) The simplicity of a single, simple loan period is gone. A book may now be used from anything from a minute to a year. This usage comes in two main forms: usage inside the library ('reference' or 'in-library' use), which involves the book being off the shelves for a few hours at most; and borrowing that may result in the book being absent from the shelves anything from a day to several months. There are normally different categories of users that have different loan privileges and so, conceivably, different borrowing habits.

(ii) Data are more difficult to collect: it is not practical to record unsatisfied demand or 'in-library' use for individual titles, except in special circumstances, in which devices such as transparent filaments can be used. The only readily available data are the loan records in the form of dates stamped on date due labels and the slips of paper upon which individual loans are recorded.

(iii) Reservations are important and so, too, are the procedures for recalling from loan books that have been reserved. Reservations and recalls play an ambivalent role in library stock management. On the one hand, they are a fail-safe device to mitigate the consequences of failure to find a book and, therefore, lessen the importance of maintaining a high degree of availability. On the other hand, they are singularly time-consuming in terms of labour.

In view of this complexity and the limitations of the mathematical theory of queues, it was decided to use Monte Carlo simulation* in the following manner.

The borrowing process was described in terms of a flow-chart in which the logical consequences or alternative actions were specified. The logic diagram eventually used is reproduced as Fig. 5.1.

At various points it is necessary to specify numerical data. This can be a fixed amount as, for example, the number of copies provided. Sometimes, however, it will be a probability, as, for example, in the case of in-library use compared with borrowing. There may be some long-term

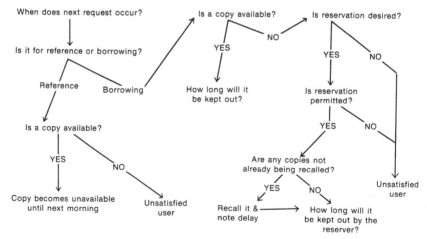

Fig. 5.1.   Logic diagram of the borrowing process.

*The following paragraphs explain what was done. For further details on this technique, reference should be made to textbooks on operations research.

probability that the next reader to find a book will use it in the library instead of borrowing it, but no *certainty* as to which the next reader will do. In a simulation, this can be represented by sampling random numbers within a predetermined range. Each number can have a particular outcome pre-assigned to it. The assignment of outcomes to numbers will have been based on the assumed probabilities of the various outcomes. For example, if two-thirds of book consultations took place in the library and the remaining one-third involved borrowing and if a dice were used to select random numbers, then numbers 1, 2, 3 and 4 could represent in-library use and 5 and 6 represent borrowing. By rolling the dice to determine the nature of each simulated consultation as it occurred, not only would a life-like uncertainty be preserved, but also an overall long-term pattern conforming to the actual pattern in the library of two-thirds in-library use and one-third borrowing.

Some decisions are determined within the system. For example, whether or not a copy of the book is currently available depends on whether or not a previous reader is still using it. When successive requests occur can be determined by a predetermined sequence or by sampling random numbers to determine inter-arrival intervals.

The empirical approach has four significant advantages:

(i) Computers can be programmed to perform a prodigious amount of simulation in a short time.

(ii) It is possible in this manner to simulate situations of great complexity so long as the situation can be described in logical and probabilistic terms.

(iii) It is convenient to perform 'sensitivity analyses', whereby a series of simulations can be performed with a succession of changes in the values of a particular parameter to observe how significantly the changes affect the overall performance of the system being studied. This can indicate whether or not precision is required in measuring that particular parameter.

(iv) The mathematical skills required to use Monte Carlo simulation are small.

In the spring of 1969, a computer program* was written to perform a simulation based on the logic diagram in Fig. 5.1. This required the following data to be specified:

*For formal documentation of the program and a listing of the program itself, see Appendix A2 of Buckland *et al.*[52]

(i) The number of requests to be simulated.

(ii) The number of copies of the book.

(iii) A maximum allowable number of reservations accepted for one book.

(iv) The pattern of demand expressed as a distribution of intervals between requests.

(v) The ratio of borrowing to 'in-library' use.

(vi) The loan period defined by a distribution of return times.

(vii) The probability that a would-be borrower will make a reservation if a copy is not immediately available.

(viii) The delays involved in recalls.

The computer was programmed to report the following results:

For 'in-library' use:

(a) The number of 'in-library' requests made.

(b) The percentage of 'in-library' requests that were satisfied.

For borrowing use:

(a) The number of borrowing requests.

(b) The percentage of borrowing requests satisfied either immediately or after a reservation.

(c) The level of immediate availability (i.e. the percentage of borrowing demands that were satisfied immediately).

(d) The pattern of delays experienced following reservation.

Early in 1969 a series of 60 simulations were performed on data relating to the University of Lancaster Library and the results will be described in Chapter 7.

D. SUMMARY

The considerable variation in loan policies appears to derive from conflicting objectives. There is a basic relationship between

—level of demand,

—number of copies,

—loan period, and

—immediate availability.

The cardinal rule of library stock control is that both the loan period and the duplication policy should be related to the level of demand for the title and to each other.

Analytical approaches including the mathematical theory of queues can be used to quantify the relationships involved, but Monte Carlo simulation is a more practical approach to the complexities of libraries.

CHAPTER 6

The Relationship between Borrowing Habits and Official Loan Regulations

So far we have referred more or less vaguely to the 'loan period' meaning the length of time that a book is off the shelf. This can, perhaps, be more accurately defined as a 'retention time'. Clearly, it is the retention time that is important in determining immediate availability. However, the retention time is not directly under the control of the librarian. It is true that library staff can ensure that books are reshelved promptly after a borrower has returned them, but this is of limited significance compared with the length of time the borrower retains the book. What the librarian *can* control are three regulations, which, together, constitute a loan policy:

(i) The official loan period for a given category of user: that is, the time by the end of which a borrower is required to return or renew a loan.

(ii) The number of renewals permitted. Usually unlimited renewals are allowed but sometimes this is restricted to one or none—a restriction that sometimes stems from administrative aspects of the procedures for maintaining loan records.

(iii) The maximum number of books that a borrower may have out on loan at any given time.

Because retention times are what matter (both in reality and, therefore, in simulation), it is important to examine what relationship there may be between the loan policies that the librarian can control and the retention times. It is remarkable that this very important topic appears to have been almost completely ignored until about 1968.

A. THE RELATIONSHIP BETWEEN THE OFFICIAL LOAN PERIOD AND RETENTION TIMES

The factors that seem likely to affect the length of time that a book is retained are numerous and varied: the subject, level and type of the book; the subject background, work habits, spending-power and motivation of the borrower; the thousand and one possible distractions that might affect his behaviour (including recall notices); and the official loan period. In a situation where the factors involved are of such complexity, one might expect books to be returned as if at random—of all books borrowed on a given day, a small percentage of those still out being returned each day—with perhaps a small peak for returns and renewals at the expiry of the loan period. In order to examine this aspect of librarianship and following trial data collection in 1967, enquiries were made concerning the loan regulations and loan recording systems of most British university libraries. Subsequently, Manchester, Strathclyde and Sussex were asked for additional data because the discharged issue slips of these libraries were convenient to handle and represented a suitable range of loan periods and subject interests.

Daily bundles of discharged slips were collected as follows:

Manchester: All discharged slips from the Main Library, 10–15 March 1969.

Strathclyde: All discharged slips from the Andersonian Library, 3–15 February 1969.

Sussex: All discharged two-week loans by undergraduates from the main library, 14–27 February 1969.

The slips were analysed as follows:

(i) Procedures (ii)–(ix) below were conducted quite separately for each of the daily bundles of discharged slips.

(ii) Each slip was stamped with the date of return as a precautionary measure.

(iii) Each daily bundle was sorted into categories according to the official loan period and whether or not there had been a reservation. For example, for Strathclyde there were four categories:

4-week loans (Staff and Postgraduates)*: No reservation

---

*The term 'postgraduate' is used here and throughout in its British meaning: students pursuing higher degrees such as M.A., M.Sc. and Ph.D. In the United States, the corresponding term is 'graduate student'.

4-week loans (Staff and Postgraduates): Reservation
2-week loans (Undergraduates): No reservation
2-week loans (Undergraduates): Reservation

(iv) Procedures (v)–(viii) below were conducted quite separately for each category.

(v) Each category was then sorted by the number of times (if any) that the loan had been renewed and the number of loans renewed 0, 1, 2, 3, . . . times was counted. These data were required for consideration of the relationship between official loan period and frequency renewal. They will be considered in the discussion of this topic in the next section.

(vi) Slips representing loans that were *not* renewed were sorted by date of borrowing. The distribution of lengths of loan was calculated by counting the number of slips relating to each date of borrowing and by comparing the date of borrowing with the date of return. An item borrowed and then returned *on the same day* was regarded as having been retained for 0 days. An item borrowed one day and returned the next day was regarded as having been kept out for 1 day, and so on.

(vii) Slips relating to loans that had been renewed *one or more times* were sorted by date of original borrowing in order to establish the distribution of lengths of loan between original borrowing and final return. The procedure was the same as (vi) above.

(viii) In order to examine the length of time books were retained after the final renewal of loan, the slips relating to loans that had been renewed *one or more times* were re-sorted by date of final renewal in order to establish the distribution of the lengths of time between final renewal and final return. The procedure was the same as in (vi) above.

(ix) The frequency of actual length of loan (derived from (vi)–(viii)) for each daily bundle of discharged slips was summed within each category.

All analyses were performed manually except in the case of Sussex two-week loans for which the slips were in the form of 80 column Hollerith cards and were already partially punched. For these, procedures (vi) and (viii) were performed by computer using a specially prepared program, and procedure (vii) was not possible. In the case of Strathclyde, a further analysis was made of the borrowing of science literature as defined by classes 5: Pure sciences and 6: Applied sciences of the

Universal Decimal Classification. In addition, data relating to the University of Michigan had been published by Burkhalter[54] and the University of Strathclyde Library kindly made available data collected there in earlier years. In the spring of 1971, Mr. M. G. Ford kindly supplied comparable data relating to one-week borrowing at the Wills Memorial Library, University of Bristol.

Data collection at Lancaster posed a particular problem because all loans were of the 'fixed return date' type, namely 'until the end of term' and 'until the end of the year'. This means that the length of the official loan period changes daily, in contrast to the 'fixed loan period' policies of the other data. In principle, one could pick a single day at a specified length of time before the books were due back and analyse how long these books were kept out. Unfortunately, too few items were borrowed each day to permit a meaningful analysis, so two exploratory investigations were performed on the discharged issue slips that had been collected for a complete academic year: 1967–1968. It should be noted that renewals were treated as fresh loans, because they could not be distinguished.

(a) A random sample of one in twenty slips was drawn. The length of time between borrowing and return or renewal was measured and expressed not in days, but as a fraction of the length of time between the date of borrowing and the date due back, thus:

$$\text{Retention factor} = \frac{\text{Length of time kept out}}{\substack{\text{Length of time between date of} \\ \text{borrowing and date due back.}}}$$

This manipulation had a normalising effect in that any tendency to return books when they were due back would be reflected by a peaking in the distribution of retention factors around the value of 1. It permitted data on loans of different borrowing dates to be aggregated.

(b) An attempt was made to produce a distribution comparable with those derived from libraries with fixed loan periods. This was done by resorting the data by date of borrowing and examining a group of loans made 50–56 days before the date on which they were due back. A separate analysis was made of the retention time of each of the books borrowed on each of these days. The results were then aggregated into the following classes.

		Observations	
Kept out	0– 7 days	718	(25%)
Kept out	8–14 days	347	(12%)
Kept out	15–21 days	270	(9%)

Observations

Kept out	22–28 days	212	(7%)
Kept out	29–35 days	193	(7%)
Kept out	36–42 days	164	(6%)
Kept out	43–49 days	220	(8%)
Kept out	50–56 days	651	(23%)
Kept out	over 56 days	92	(3%)

Since, by definition, all the data related to books borrowed 50–56 days before the date on which they were due back, all data were due for return in the 50–56 day class. Any tendency for books to be returned when they are due back would be reflected by a peak in the histogram at this point.

The data collected are summarised graphically in Figs. 6.1 and 6.2. *They show quite clearly that there is a marked tendency for borrowed books to be returned (or renewed) when they are due back and that this pattern is strongly marked regardless of the length of the official loan period, the status of the borrower or the subject matter of the books borrowed.* The negative exponential pattern assumed by Morse[155], if it exists at all, must have a very shallow slope, which only emerges in the case of very long official loan periods. For practical purposes, the distribution is dominated by the peak when the books are due for return or renewal.

This pattern is not unfamiliar to librarians accustomed to using the Browne issue records formerly common in public libraries, but the strength of its 'peakiness' is not widely appreciated. The only other published data on this known to the author is that published by Burkhalter[54] in 1968 and Clinton[58] in 1972. Burkhalter should be respected for pioneering but, in the author's view, his interpretation was mistaken. Data were collected only for one official loan period: material borrowed by undergraduates and graduates for two weeks at the University of Michigan Library. The result is indicated by the top right-hand graph on Fig. 6.1. The interpretation was that because so much material was kept for a full two weeks, this was evidence that the material was needed for longer and a change to a three-week loan period was recommended. If he had collected data on other official loan periods, it would probably have been clear that changing the official loan period moves the peak. If a peak is taken as evidence that the official loan period is too short, then we should get an endless lengthening of loan periods. Burkhalter mentions but did not stress the effect of changing from two to three weeks in reducing immediate availability.

In conclusion, the power of the librarian to determine an official loan period gives him an extremely precise control device for influencing the

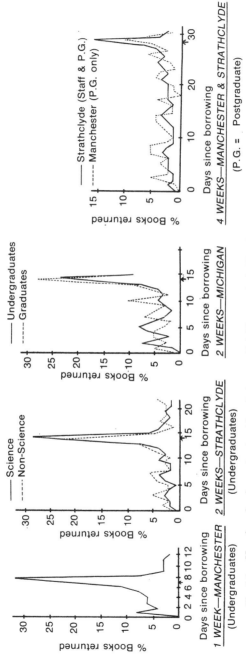

Fig. 6.1. How long books are kept out in relation to official loan period. (Graphs show the percentage of books returned on successive days since they were borrowed. Data from Manchester and Strathclyde exclude renewals and items reserved by other readers. See Appendix B for these and additional data.)

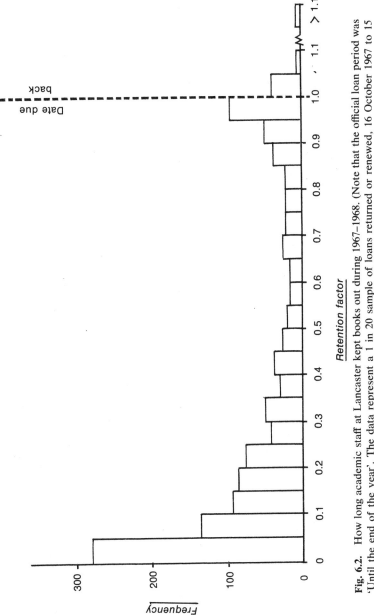

Fig. 6.2. How long academic staff at Lancaster kept books out during 1967–1968. (Note that the official loan period was 'Until the end of the year'. The data represent a 1 in 20 sample of loans returned or renewed, 16 October 1967 to 15 October 1968. The retention factor is the time kept out expressed as a proportion of the time allowed out.)

retention times of his borrowers and thereby the immediate availability of his books *unless* this is counteracted by changes in the probability of renewals.

B. THE RELATIONSHIP BETWEEN THE OFFICIAL LOAN PERIOD AND FREQUENCY OF RENEWAL

The data presented in the previous section would suggest that if a librarian wished to increase the immediate availability of books in his library, he might do well to consider shortening official loan periods because of the fairly direct effect this would have on retention times and, thereby, on immediate availability. However, received opinion appeared to be that shorter loan periods would simply cause more frequent renewal. The net result could, therefore, be unchanged overall retention times (i.e. from initial borrowing to final return) but with increased bureaucratic inconvenience to both librarian and borrower on account of the greater frequency of the administrative process of renewal.

However, in the absence of any known examination of the facts of this important factor, loan records were analysed early in 1969 in two different ways.

B1. Frequency of Renewal at Libraries with a Fixed Loan Period

All the data from libraries other than Lancaster that were analysed with respect to retention times contained information about renewals. In each case, renewal was effected by stamping a new 'date due back' on the loan slip. Consequently, the number of additional dates stamped on the cards indicated the number of renewals and all slips were analysed in this respect. The results are tabulated in Fig. 6.3.

The initial impression of the data is one of broad similarity. Closer inspection shows that the probability of renewal appears to vary more between institutions than within them, for example, the probability of zero renewals at Manchester is undergraduates 67%; postgraduates 69%;—at Strathclyde undergraduates 81%; staff and postgraduates 76%. Two sets of data are exceptional and, in the event, derive from exceptional situations. In the case of undergraduates at Sussex, only one renewal was permitted and the procedure involved a little more inconvenience than in the other examples. Here the proportion not renewed is unusually high. In the case of teaching staff at Manchester, the data are particularly interesting. At that time the loan records for teaching staff

LOAN PERIOD	No. of loans analysed	FREQUENCY OF RENEWAL %					
		0	1	2	3	4	5+
1 WEEK: Undergraduates at Manchester	2,115	67	19	7	4	1	2
2 WEEKS: Undergraduates at Strathclyde							
—Science	888	78	11	3	3	1	2
—Non-Science	1,208	83	12	2	1	0.8	0.8
—Combined	2,096	81	11	13	2	1	2
Undergraduates at Sussex	7,154	c95	c5	Only one renewal allowed			
4 WEEKS: P.G. at Manchester	307	69	17	6	2	2	3
Staff at Manchester	306	c24	c42	c12	c6	c6	c10
		Renewed automatically until end of session					
Staff & P.G. at Strathclyde							
—Science	510	70	12	6	4	2	6
—Non-Science	483	81	10	4	5	0.2	0.2
—Combined	993	76	11	5	4	1	3

Fig. 6.3. Frequency of renewal in relation to the official loan period. (The data from Strathclyde, which excludes journals, was regarded as 'Science' if it had been classified in U.D.C. classes 5 or 6. 'Non-Science' data refers to the remaining classes. Data excludes items reserved by other users whilst out on loan. P.G. = Postgraduates.)

were automatically renewed until the end of the session (or the prior return of the book) without any action on the borrowers' part. On this basis, there is an exceptionally large number of 'renewals'. Although the loan period was officially four weeks for teaching staff, the data on retention times are more characteristic of a situation with an 'until the end of the session' loan period which, so far as the borrowers were concerned, the policy effectively was.

Science borrowing was looked at by means of separate analyses of science and non-science books at Strathclyde. There is very little difference in the case of undergraduates, but more in the case of postgraduates and teaching staff. The numbers involved are, however, fairly small.

The conclusion is that although there is some variation in the frequency of renewal, the effect of the length of the official loan period cannot be of much importance.

B2. Frequency of Renewal at Lancaster

An 'until the end of term' type loan period was in force at Lancaster for undergraduate borrowers in the spring of 1969. Given the tendency noted above for books to be returned only when they are due back, there is a flurry of books being returned or renewed at the end of each term. The books could have been borrowed at any time since the previous end of term.

When a book was returned, the loan record (a 5 in. × 3 in. slip imprinted by Bookamatic embossed cards with details of the loan) was removed from the file and thrown away. Since renewals were treated as fresh loans, the 'return' procedure was followed and the old slip thrown away and fresh record made. It was decided to examine the relationship (if any) between the length of time a book had been out and the probability that the loan would be renewed. This was possible because the loans being returned (or renewed) could have been borrowed at any time during the term—an effective range of nearly nine weeks—and because the staff at the Service Desk kindly agreed to use two clearly marked waste bins. Discharged slips relating to loans that had been renewed were put in one waste bin and the discharged slips relating to loans that had been returned and *not* renewed were put in the other. These slips were recovered and sorted by date of borrowing. The results are shown in Fig. 6.4. Working

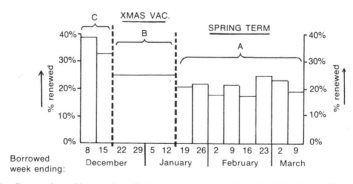

Fig. 6.4.   Proportion of borrowings that were renewed at the end of the Spring Term 1969 at Lancaster in relation to the date of borrowing.

from right to left, this graph falls into three parts:

A: Items borrowed during the Spring Term. These will all be original borrowings and the proportion renewed as opposed to returned at the end of term remains fairly stable. This indicates that for material kept out until the end of term, the probability of renewal is influenced little if at all by the length of loan period.

B: Items borrowed during the Christmas Vacation. These books were due back at the end of the Spring Term, but the amount of data involved is small and is probably best ignored. The four weeks have been averaged.

C: Items borrowed at the end of the previous term. A relatively high proportion of these loans were renewed. It should be remembered that a large proportion, perhaps 70%, of these relate to loans *renewed* at the end of the Autumn Term. This result is in keeping with the principle that once a loan has been renewed once, the probability of its being renewed again increases.

Two comments can be made on the Lancaster data:

(a) It should be remembered that the data is derived from books kept out until the end of term. Some books will already have been returned during the term—especially if borrowed early in the term. No renewals were necessary (or permitted) during the term. Consequently the graph, in excluding books returned during term, may well mask a tendency (probably fairly small) for the probability of renewal to decrease as the time kept out increases.

(b) The data were collected during a period of intense activity at the Service Desk. The staff were under considerable strain and could well have sometimes thrown slips into the wrong bin, although a hasty spot check suggested that they were, in fact, very reliable. If slips had been thrown into the wrong bin, it might have affected the *overall* proportion apparently renewed but not the relationship between length of loan and probability of renewal that was under investigation.

Conclusion

Collecting data on the relationship between official loan period and the frequency of renewal is an inconvenient occupation in the context of manual loan recording systems. *The data presented above indicate that the frequency of renewal is affected little or not at all by the length of the official loan period.*

C. THE RELATIONSHIP BETWEEN RETENTION TIMES AND LIMITATIONS ON THE NUMBER OF LOANS PERMITTED TO AN INDIVIDUAL BORROWER

At the University of Lancaster Library as at all the other libraries surveyed, the official loan regulations prescribe that borrowers must not have more than a certain number of books out on loan at a given time. At Lancaster, and, one suspects, at the other libraries, these regulations are not enforced except in exceptional circumstances. The reason lies in the administrative details of the manner in which loans are recorded. In each case, loans are recorded on slips of paper or card. To enforce a limitation on the number of loans out to any individual means that a file of loan records arranged by the borrower's name has to be maintained and checked—a laborious business. Performing a spot check on a file arranged by any other order is an unattractive proposition.

In most university libraries, the regulations exist unenforced because the benefits are not considered worth the effort at service desks, which often have more than enough work anyway.

In some loan-recording systems, such as Browne, borrowers deposit a ticket (or envelope) each time they borrow a book. The ticket is given back when the book is returned. In such circumstances, the maximum number of books out on loan is effectively regulated by the number of tickets issued. However, these systems are uncommon in university libraries and becoming less common in other kinds of library. Consequently, this type of control cannot be used. Computer-aided issue systems, however, which are being introduced, restore the ability to enforce this kind of restriction.

In these circumstances, there was little incentive to explore this relationship. Nevertheless, this relationship is well worth examining because some universities, such as Birmingham, Leeds and University College, London do, or did, place considerable reliance on the enforcement of this limitation in maintaining the immediate availability of their book stocks. Furthermore, a distinct impression was gained that other libraries would begin to enforce this type of regulation as soon as improved computer-based technology made it convenient to enforce. It therefore seems apposite to consider the effects of such a policy, especially as no previous treatment of this topic has been found.

C1. How Low Should the Maximum be Set?

It would seem reasonable that there should be some fairly high maximum in order to stop any thoroughly anti-social hoarders who might be tempted to remove whole sections of books *en bloc*. How high the maximum should be for this purpose is not clear—perhaps 30? However, the limitation is usually enforced for a rather different reason: to induce borrowers to return books. Once they have reached the limit, they cannot borrow any more until they bring some back. Where should the limit be set?—at 4?—or 6? Here a dilemma is posed by the great variation between individuals in borrowing, especially undergraduates. Data relating to the University of Leeds published by Page and Tucker[174] showed the annual number of loans per student was distributed thus

26·1%	of students borrowed	no books at all	in a year
4·5%	of students borrowed	only one book	in a year
3·7%	of students borrowed	2 books	in a year
3·5%	of students borrowed	3 books	in a year
37·8%	of students borrowed	3 or less books	in a year

Given that there was a two-week official loan period with renewals permitted, it is clear if borrowing was fairly evenly spread throughout the year, only a small minority of students (and, therefore, of loans) are likely to have been affected by a limit set at 6—or even 4 books out at one time. It is also clear that it is only the 'good' library borrowers—those that wish to use library books—that are likely to be inconvenienced by this limit. Accepting that the incidence of this rule is highly selective, we must also enquire how efficient it is.

C2. Which Books are Returned?

In such a situation, the borrower is normally free to choose *which* books are returned. Some books are in heavy demand and it is these that ought to be returned if levels of immediate availability are to be maintained—and the frustration of other would-be borrowers minimised. Other books are so rarely used that it makes little difference to other library users whether or not they are returned. Which books are returned when a borrower has to return some in order to borrow more? One suspects (and discussions have tended to confirm) that there is a tendency for borrowers to retain the more popular and more strongly recommended books and to return less popular, fringe material. If this is the case, then as a policy designed to maintain immediate availability, it is clearly inefficient.

There is little doubt that a limitation on the number of books allowed out at any given time *will* have some effect in reducing retention times by inducing early returns and less renewal. Other aspects are, however, less attractive. It is of uncertain effect unless the limit is quite low; it inconveniences the keen library users most; and it is of doubtful efficiency in that the more popular books may well stay out longer than the less popular books.

D.   SUMMARY ON THE RELATIONSHIP BETWEEN LOAN REGULATIONS AND RETENTION TIMES

The significance of these findings on the relationship between retention times, frequency of renewal and official loan periods is considerable. *They mean that the librarian has, in his ability to determine official loan periods, a powerful and precise control mechanism for influencing the availability of the books in his library.* In terms of the previous chapter, they permit us to predict the retention times likely to be associated with any given official loan period—thereby permitting us to calculate the consequences of changes in official loan periods with some confidence.

CHAPTER 7

The Appraisal and Revision of Loan Regulations: A Case Study

A. INTRODUCTION

In Chapter 5, Section A, the basic relationships for individual titles between demand, retention times, number of copies and immediate availability were described. In Sections B and C, techniques were presented that permit numerical calculations to be made concerning the precise interactions between these factors. In Chapter 6, it was shown that it was possible to estimate the distribution of retention times associated with different official loan periods. By the process of substituting a selection of different distributions of retention times corresponding to a number of different official loan periods, it becomes possible to estimate the likely consequences of adopting different official loan periods on the immediate availability of books at any given level of demand. By the same means, estimates can be made of other variations in the factors involved, such as the level (and inter-arrival distribution) of demand, and the number of copies.

B. A CASE STUDY

During 1969 the loan regulations at the University of Lancaster Library were examined.

It is clearly inappropriate to think in terms of individual titles in a library that had some 100,000 volumes and was growing fast. The necessary further development was to transfer the emphasis from individual titles to the whole collection—in this case, the books on the open shelves. That is, the whole library stock excluding a few specialist categories, notably the Short Loan reserve collection, the rare books collection and some rarely used and partially processed books kept in a basement stack. Two actions were necessary: first, to examine the actual distribution of demand between titles and second, to achieve some meaningful overall measures of performance.

B1. The Distribution of Demand

Data were collected by examining date due labels. In order to pick a sample, the library classification scheme was divided into its conventional divisions each denoting a 'subject'. The divisions were numbered 1–25 and random numbers used to pick five 'subjects'. These were, in terms of the Bliss Bibliographic classification:

> AL   Logic
> C   Chemistry
> N   History of the Americas
> T   Economics and business studies
> W   Linguistics.

The list of books in the library in these categories (the 'Shelf list') was then used and the dates stamped during one year on the date due label of every tenth item on the list were counted. For the most part, the volumes were on the shelves. These posed no problem. Those not on the shelves were searched for elsewhere. Many were out on loan and these were examined as they were returned. Some were on Short Loan; others were missing. The shelf lists contain one entry for each edition. In the relatively few cases where there was more than one copy or more than one volume, one only, selected at random, was examined. The following categories were excluded:

(i) All serials. These pose particular problems in sampling. 'Title' and 'edition' are not useful units. Consideration was deferred.
(ii) Dates on date due labels that refer to use in the Short Loan collection were ignored.
(iii) Books that had been in the library for less than a year were excluded.

This data collection was carried out under considerable pressure to achieve completed recommendations by a specified date. In the event, 757 of the sample of 876 were found, the remaining 119 were missing or did not return from loan in time. The results were as follows:

Analysis of Borrowing Histories, 1967–1968

No. of issues	0	1	2	3	4	5	6	7	8	9	10
Frequency	375	168	103	43	40	15	6	2	1	1	1
%	50	22	14	6	5	2	1	—	—	—	—

At this point we come up against a major problem. These data refer to *satisfied* demand—actual loans—not to the demand itself. To establish the total demand, one needs to know both satisfied *and* unsatisfied demand, but in an open-access collection the latter cannot easily be assessed. It is, therefore, necessary to deduce the total demand from the satisfied demand.

The total demand and the satisfied demand are clearly identical when total demand is zero. They will always be identical if, in the event of a book not being immediately available, a reservation is *always* made—unless a chronic queue of reservations develops. It was quite clear that reservations were being made on only a small fraction of the occasions when a book could not be found. Given that reservations were not usually made, it follows that the total demand and the satisfied demand will diverge as total demand increases, if the number of copies and the retention times remain constant. This is because as total demand rises, the immediate availability decreases. Since the satisfied demand depends primarily on the immediate availability, it too will constitute a progressively smaller proportion of total demand. Given that the total demand diverges from satisfied demand as both increase, the data collected imply that the library's books are subject to a demand that is similar to the Bradford–Zipf distribution.

Table 7.1.

Popularity class	Level of total demand (Demands per time period T)	Proportion of book stock	Proportion of demand
A	$4\frac{1}{2}+$	3%	38%
B	$3\frac{1}{2}-4\frac{1}{2}$	6%	27%
C	$2\frac{1}{2}-3\frac{1}{2}$	10%	19%
D	$1\frac{1}{2}-2\frac{1}{2}$	17%	12%
E	$\frac{1}{2}-1\frac{1}{2}$	24%	4%
F	$0-\frac{1}{2}$	40%	0%

The curve that seemed most likely to represent the distribution of total demand was plotted graphically. Six levels of demand ('popularity classes') were defined. The proportion of the book stock in each popularity class and the proportion of demand accounted for by the books in each popularity class were estimated from the graph. The estimates are presented in Table 7.1.

B2. The Calculation of Immediate Availabilities

Experimental simulations as outlined in Chapter 5, Section B, were performed using distributions of retention times associated with official loan periods of one, two, five and ten weeks. (Subsequently, more accurate data on retention times led to the revision of the more important results, that are shown in Table 7.2.)

POPU-LARITY CLASS	ONE COPY Loan Policy				TWO COPIES Loan Policy				THREE COPIES Loan Policy			
	(i)	(ii)	(iii)	(iv)	(i)	(ii)	(iii)	(iv)	(i)	(ii)	(iii)	(iv)
A	91	79	52	37	100	98	84	66	100	100	97	86
B	94	86	62	44	100	99	91	77	100	100	99	93
C	98	94	72	56	100	100	97	87	100	100	100	98
D	99	98	82	68	100	100	99	84	100	100	100	100
E	100	100	97	85	100	100	100	100	100	100	100	100

This table shows simulation results showing immediate availability (%) for 60 trials: 5 popularity classes $A-E \times 4$ loan policies, (i)–(iv) $\times 3$ levels of duplication. The four loan policies correspond approximately to loan periods of one week, two weeks, five weeks and ten weeks, respectively. There was no point in simulating popularity class F because the level of demand is so low that immediate availability is certain to be close to 100% in all cases. The table should be read as follows: a title in popularity class A would have a 91% chance of being available when sought if the loan period is one week and only one copy is held.

The five-week official loan period (iii) was included because it approximates to the 'until the end of term' loan period then in force at Lancaster.

Before the implications of these calculations are examined, it is appropriate to consider measures of performance to be used in comparing loan policies.

B3. Measures of Library Performance

Immediate Availability.   So far we have only discussed one measure of performance: immediate availability. This is the probability that a copy of *a given book* will be immediately available on the shelf when sought.

Satisfaction Level.   For practical purposes, it is the overall performance that matters—the overall availability of the collection as a whole *in relation to the pattern of demand on it.* The concept of *Satisfaction Level* was therefore defined as the proportion of demands that are satisfied immediately—all demands, that is. This is, in fact, the weighted mean immediate availability where the weighting is the proportion of demand falling on a given book. It is important not to confuse Satisfaction Level with unweighted mean immediate availability. The difference can be illustrated as follows. Suppose a science library of 100,000 volumes was increased by an additional 100,000 volumes of oriental literature that was of no interest whatsoever to the users of the science library. The demand for the additional 100,000 would be virtually zero and the immediate availability of the volumes concerned would be effectively 100%. The impact of this additional 100,000 would be to increase considerably the unweighted mean immediate availability of the collection as a whole, but because there was no demand for this material, the Satisfaction Level would remain unaffected.

Collection Bias.   So far discussion has been in terms of readers seeking books, yet library use is often less directed than this. People browse more or less purposefully. Little is known about browsing but it is clearly of some importance. Let us consider what happens in a typical university library when a user looks vaguely for a book, any book, on, say, economics. Supposing he reaches the section of the library devoted to economics, he will be faced by an array of books. What are the characteristics of this array? In the first place, the library staff will probably have removed all the strongly recommended books and put them in a reserve collection—probably on closed access out of the reach of browsers. In the second place, other popular or recommended books will very likely already be out on loan to other library users. Some proportion of less popular books will also be out on loan. Since, for any given official loan period, immediate availability increases as the demand decreases, we can expect a large proportion of the unpopular, unrecommended books to be present in the array. These are the books that, in every library, appear to remain unused year in year out. In other words, the array of books available to the browser tends to be *systematically biased* in favour of the less popular and the less recommended. We define this tendency as *Collection Bias* and it is measurable. It is, in effect, the difference in immediate availability between popular books and unpopular books. The most unpopular books are always 100% immediately available and so one convenient measure is the proportion of the 10% most popular books that is usually off the shelves. It is difficult to be more explicit but Collection Bias appears to be a disservice to library users. It cannot be entirely eliminated except in a chained library, but it would seem prudent to attempt to reduce it.

We assume therefore, that a good library service should have a high Satisfaction Level and a low Collection Bias.

B4. Diagnosis at Lancaster and a Test

It is appropriate at this point to return to our calculations. We know the distribution of books in relation to the levels of demand and we have estimated the immediate availability associated with some combinations of popularity class, official loan period and number of copies.

The data that are important for the rest of this section are summarised in Table 7.2. Section 1 summarises data on the distribution of demand. Section 2 summarises calculations of immediate availability. Section 3.1 expresses the distribution of demand in terms of 1,000 books. Sections 3.2–3.4 show the estimated effect of various loan periods on the 1,000 books, expressed as the number of them in each popularity class that could be expected to be on the shelves (i.e. immediately available).

This last line of Table 7.2 offers a check on the validity of the various assumptions and calculations. If a five-week official loan period approximates to the loan policies in force in Lancaster at the time, if the assumptions about the level and distribution of demand are correct and if the simulation is a valid replication of the borrowing process, then at the mid-point of the 1967–1968 session the number of books out on loan ought to be 12%, namely 122 per thousand because it is calculated that 878 per thousand will *not* be on loan.

Sufficient data had been collected relating to 1967–1968 to permit an independent estimate based on issue records and the analysis of discharged issue slips. This produced an estimate of 12%. This was considered to be an adequate validation of the calculations.

Satisfaction Level is the weighted mean immediate availability, the weighting being the proportion of demand for a given book. Since we have made no distinction between books in the same popularity class, this

Table 7.2.

1. Demand data Popularity class:	A	B	C	D	E	F	Total
1.1 Distribution of demand (d_i):	0·38	0·27	0·19	0·12	0·04	0·00	1·00
1.2 Distribution of books (b_i):	0·03	0·06	0·10	0·17	0·24	0·40	1·00
2. Immediate availabilities with one copy							
2.1 —1-week official loan period (i)	0·90	0·94	0·98	0·99	1·0	1·0	—
2.2 —2-week official loan period (ii)	0·74	0·82	0·90	0·96	0·99	1·0	—
2.3 —5-week official loan period (iii)	0·5	0·6	0·7	0·8	0·92	1·0	—
3. Implications of A and B							
3.1 How 1,000 books would be distributed (from 1.2)	30	60	100	170	240	400	1,000
How many of these 1,000 books would be on shelves? (from 3.1 and 2.1–2.3, respectively)							
3.2 —1-week official loan period (i)	27	56	98	168	240	400	989
3.3 —2-week official loan period (ii)	22	49	90	163	238	400	962
3.4 —5-week official loan period (iii)	15	36	70	136	221	400	878

becomes the mean of the immediate availability for each class multiplied by the probability that a demand will be for that class. With a one-week official loan period this becomes:

Popularity class	Distribution of demand d (1.1 in Table 7.2)		Immediate availability (2.1 in Table 7.2)		Probability that a demand will be for an item in this popularity class *and* that it will be satisfied immediately
A	0·38	×	0·90	=	0·34
B	0·27	×	0·94	=	0·25
C	0·19	×	0·98	=	0·19
D	0·12	×	0·99	=	0·12
E	0·04	×	1·00	=	0·04
F	0·0	×	1·00	=	0·00
Therefore, overall Satisfaction Level is					0·94

The right-hand column can be supplied for each loan period to give an 'availability table' thus:

Popularity class	Official loan period		
	1 week	2 weeks	5 weeks
A (3% books)	0·34	0·28	0·19
B (6% books)	0·25	0·22	0·16
C (10% books)	0·19	0·17	0·13
D (17% books)	0·12	0·12	0·10
D (24% books)	0·04	0·04	0·04
F (40% books)	0·00	0·00	0·00
Satisfaction Level	0·94	0·83	0·62

Each cell gives the probability that a demand will be for a book in that popularity class and that it will be satisfied with that loan period.

It will be observed that the figures indicate that in 1967–1968, a person seeking a book in the University of Lancaster Library had only a 0·6 chance of finding it. If, however, there had been a two-week loan period in force with the demand as it then was, the chance would have been 0·83 and with a one-week loan period it would have been 0·94.

However, we now re-examine this availability table in the light of the cardinal rule of library stock control ('that the loan period should be inversely related to the level of demand') and consider the effects of different official loan periods for different popularity levels. Suppose, for example that

    classes A and B had a one-week loan period
    classes C and D had a two-week loan period
and classes E and F had a five-week loan period (or 'end of term').

In this case by adding the appropriate cells, the Satisfaction Level becomes $0·34 + 0·25 + 0·17 + 0·12 + 0·04 + 0·0 = 0·92$, but note that only 9% of the books and 59% of the loans involve the relative inconvenience of a one-week official loan period.

Another example involving only two different loan periods might be classes A, B and C at two weeks and the rest at five (or 'end of term') this would give a Satisfaction Level of $0·28 + 0·22 + 0·17 + 0·10 + 0·04 + 0·00 = 0·81$.

Collection Bias can be most simply calculated from Table 7.2. The number of books in popularity classes A and B (the 9% most popular) was 90 per thousand. The number expected to be on the shelves with a one-week loan period is $27 + 56 = 83$. Therefore, the number absent is $90 - 83 = 7$ and the proportion absent (the 'Collection Bias') is $7/90$ or approximately 8%. The Collection Bias with the five-week official loan period is 43%. Note that different means of achieving a given Satisfaction Level can have different effects on the Collection Bias.

A variety of calculations were performed in order to assess alternative loan policies including the possibility of increasing the number of copies instead of or in combination with changes in loan periods.

It became quite clear that, if feasible, a policy of relating the official loan period directly to the level of demand was unquestionably the most effective in increasing Satisfaction Level and reducing Collection Bias with a minimum of inconvenience to the user. So far as was known, there was no technical term in librarianship for this kind of policy, so it was dubbed a 'variable loan policy'.

A memorandum advocating a variable loan policy was submitted to a library staff meeting and a period of intensive discussion of principles and practicabilities ensued. There were three problem areas:

(a) An ideal library would have 100% Satisfaction Level and 0% Collection Bias. Lancaster had 62% and 43%, respectively, which, it was agreed, was not good enough. At what level should one aim?

(b) A 'fixed' official loan period of one or two weeks as opposed to a requiring *all* books back by a given date (e.g. the end of term) would necessitate a more complicated system of recording loans and the regular sending of overdue notices. How should these administrative changes be organised and how much would they cost?

(c) How acceptable, politically, would the changeover to a variable loan policy be? The teaching staff were not accustomed to a one-week loan period.

The librarian then prepared a paper for the Library Committee, which summarised the situation. It is reproduced here because of its thoroughness. Note that some of the percentages were rounded in recognition that they were estimates. Note also that the phrase 'four periods a year' means that books should be returned or renewed at the end of each of the three terms and also at the end of the summer vacation.

Librarian's Memorandum*

LOAN POLICIES

1. For some time past many members of the Library staff have felt that its loan policies were not ideal, and in recent months this feeling has been reinforced by various suggestions from other members of the University that the periods of loan, and especially that for undergraduates, should be shortened. Accordingly the research team (Messrs. Buckland and Hindle) was asked to investigate the problem fully and report in time for the meeting of the Library Committee on 30th April. It is easy enough to formulate a new loan policy, but difficult to foresee all the potential effects of a change; detailed calculations must be made, data collected, and comparisons drawn with other institutions which have similar policies; and in the end some kind of value judgement must be made of the benefits expected to result from a given expenditure. The following paragraphs are intended to summarise three alternative procedures, the arguments for and against each, and the reasons for their choice.

2. We have taken two basic measures of Library performance: Satisfaction Level, S, defined as the probability that a reader will find on the shelf the book which he is seeking; and Collection Bias, B, defined as that proportion of the most-heavily-used tenth of the library stock which is on loan at a given time (this is some indication of the degree of choice which a user has when seeking library material on a given topic). Both these measures are relevant, in differing ways, to library users, and an ideal solution will give a high level for the first and a low level for the second. The problem is to optimise these levels in relation to operating costs and to a fourth variable, the need for readers to use books for some undefined period of time outside the Library (clearly a reference-only library is the optimum in regard to the first three factors, but entirely neglects out-of-building use).

3. Three possible courses of action are considered:

A: No Change

Investigations of the use of long-loan stock show that at present Satisfaction Level = 60%, Bias = 45%. We consider this to be unsatisfactory, but by selection duplication (possibly costing £10,000–£15,000 initially and £2,000 annually) Satisfaction Level could be raised to about 80% and Bias reduced to 20%, which have been chosen as our immediate target.

*Library Committee, 30 April 1969. Agendum 3. LD/69/14.

*B: Staff and Graduate Students —Four Periods per Year; Undergraduates —
Two Weeks: Renewals Allowed*

This policy would give considerable improvement over policy A. Satisfaction Level = 73%, Bias = 32%; the cost would be of the order of £1,000–£1,500 per annum, mainly in additional junior staff to handle the greatly increased number of loans.

*C: "Popular" Books Issued for Two Weeks; Others for Four Periods per
Year, Irrespective of Borrower: Renewals Allowed*

This gives the most favourable result of the three schemes: Satisfaction Level = 80%, Bias = 21%; the costs are only marginally higher than those of scheme B, and there are compensating advantages, in that the results could be made self-adjusting to any reasonable level by varying the definition of "popular" (see Appendix 1).

[Another scheme, a variation on C, was afterwards added as an amendment:

*D: "Very Popular" Books Issued for One Week; Others for Four Periods per
Year, Irrespective of Borrower: Renewals Allowed*

This policy would aim at selecting the 9% of the stock, which is most heavily used and which generates 70% of borrowing. It would cost slightly less than scheme C, and would reduce the incidence of short-period borrowing for staff. Satisfaction Level = 86% and Bias = 8%.]

4. Pros and cons of the three schemes

Pro	Con
Scheme A	
No change—understood by users	Low *S* and High *B*
No additional cost	Users not content
B and *S* could both be improved by selective duplication	Peak in Desk routine work at term end
Easier control of book stock (reservations, etc.)	Improvements in *S* and *B* very expensive
Few renewals	Many reservations
Scheme B	
Simple to understand	Inflexible
Considerable improvement in *S*	Little change in *B*
Doesn't materially reduce existing privileges of staff and graduate students	Makes undergraduates less privileged
Reduces peaks at Desk	Costs more than scheme A
	More renewals

Pro	*Con*

Scheme B (Cont.)
Fewer reservations needed than in
  scheme A (50%)
Gives mechanism for reducing
  loan period for serials
Gives some information on need
  for selective duplication

Scheme C

Pro	*Con*
Gives best values for *B* and *S*	Unpopular with more selfish staff
Treats all readers alike	and postgraduates, as it removes
Reduces peaks at Desk	some of their existing privileges
Gives mechanism for reducing	Difficult to enforce 14 day return
loan period for serials	for staff
Gives more information on library	Higher number of overdue notices
use and need for selective dupli-	required
cation	High rate of renewals (25%)
Costs only marginally more than	
scheme B	
Minimum of reservation required	
Flexible	

5. All three schemes are workable: B and C require (perhaps) two extra juniors at the Desk to handle the more complicated issue records (a date file is essential) and the expected number of overdues, at least until users have adapted to the system.

The major questions remaining, under either scheme B or C, are the exact form of the issue record (a technical decision which need not concern the Committee) and the mechanism for enforcing the changed regulations, especially if scheme C is adopted and teaching staff have to return or renew a proportion of their borrowings after 14 days.

The Committee is invited to discuss the three schemes, and recommend one to Senate.

A. G. MACKENZIE

Appendix 1

Method of Identifying "Popular" Books

(a) It is known that (excluding the Short Loan collection) 20% of the Lancaster stock generates 80% of borrowing: this is in line with experience elsewhere, and indeed could almost be guessed from such knowledge as we have of undergraduate needs and habits. Unfortunately, this 20% is also used by staff and postgraduate students, so a decision rule for loan period based solely on status of borrower will not fully achieve the desired effects; in addition I can see no valid argument for maintaining what is in effect a class distinction between undergraduates and staff—both have equally real and genuine needs, different though these may seem to be in kind.

(b) This 20% of book stock would form the 'popular' section of the collection under scheme C (whether or not some or all serials should be included is a separate, but related, question). The problem remains of identifying these books.

It has been established that records of past use are the simplest and best available predictors of future use (considerably better than the unaided subjective judgement of either teachers or librarians); we have, in stamped date labels, fairly reliable records of past use which can be easily consulted for each book. The entire stock of monographs could be checked, and different date labels inserted in the 'popular' 20%, in about 6 man-weeks (junior staff); the system would be monitored once each term, and the examination and 'downgrading' of some proportion of the 20% could take perhaps 2–3 man-weeks of (mainly) junior time. New books would be automatically 'popular' until they were downgraded, unless there was initial evidence to the contrary. Service Desk staff would be responsible for upgrading, using evidence of use or reservations; but since the general trend is always in the other direction this is not very time-consuming.

Amendment. Further reflection indicates that it would be better (and certainly cheaper) to make new books initially 'unpopular' unless there were evidence to the contrary.

(c) The dividing line between popular and unpopular books for scheme C would basically be evidence of more than twice the average demand, i.e. four or more demands per year; the system can however be set to achieve other values of Bias and Satisfaction Level by changing this decision rule.

The Library Committee opted for policy 3D: that the most popular tenth of the book stock should be subject to a one-week official loan period regardless of the status of the borrower. Strictly, this applied to monographs only. The Committee deferred consideration of loan periods for serials. A large proportion of these are confined to the library and the rest are available for loan until the end of term.

C. IMPLEMENTATION OF A VARIABLE LOAN POLICY

Once it had been decided to adopt a variable loan policy, a variety of activities ensued. These illustrate some of the administrative aspects of stock control. The terminology of Lancaster has been adopted whereby one-week loans are called 'Popular Loans' and end of term loans are called 'Long Loans'.

C1. Modification of Procedures for Recording Loans

The library used, at that time, a manual circulation system in which the records of all loans were sorted, filed and discharged by hand. There was a large sequence into which all loans were filed in call number order. This had been satisfactory because it provided prompt access to the whereabouts of books out on loan. More significantly, the policy of allowing books out on loan until the end of term or of the year had made it unnecessary to maintain a file in transaction order designed to catch books newly overdue.

The introduction of a one-week loan period for some of the books posed a major complication. The existing system could not cope with the new situation whereby some books would become overdue each day. It was, therefore, necessary to modify the circulation system quite substantially in order to cope with the new loan policies.*

C2. Monitoring of Books to Determine Appropriate Loan Period

One-week loan was designated 'Popular Loan', while 'end of term' material retained its name of 'Long Loan'.

It was decided to distinguish Popular Loan books by the date label. This

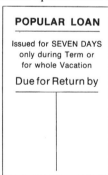

POPULAR LOAN

Issued for SEVEN DAYS
only during Term or
for whole Vacation

Due for Return by

*The Bookamatic system used embossed plastic cards resembling commercial charge cards for both book and reader. A technical description of the revised manual system can be found on pages 7.15–7.17 of Buckland[46]. *Long Loans*: These were handled as before in one sequence by call number. All became overdue on the same day. *Popular Loan*: A single slip was made and filed in call number order, but a separate sequence was created each week. Distinctively coloured stationery was associated with, and used on, different days of the week. Books becoming overdue on a particular day were indicated by, say, all blue slips in last week's file. This system is now in its turn being superseded by a computer-based system.

was made of distinctive yellow paper and, in order to accommodate plenty of date stamps, this was made larger than had been the custom. A distinctive date label serves the function of alerting the Service Desk staff to the loan period and is treated as the definitive evidence as to the loan status of the book.

It was decided to stick a distinctive marker on the spine of each Popular Loan book.

```
POP
LOAN
```

This serves two purposes:

1. To advise the potential borrower of the loan status of the book.
2. To help monitoring by identifying Popular Loan stock that would need checking for 'demotion' to Long Loan status or for duplication.

In practice, the only data that are normally available concerning the demand for individual books are the dates stamped on the date labels. It has been shown, notably in Fussler and Simon's *Patterns in the use of books in large research libraries*[80], that records of past use are comparatively reliable predictions of future use. Certainly borrowing is only a part of total demand, but because it involves a substantial absence from the shelves, it is the critically important part so far as availability is concerned. This had been confirmed experimentally by trying out on the simulation model various different assumptions about the amount of in-library use. Quite wide variations made relatively little impact on immediate availability.

In monitoring the stock to identify the top 10%, some guidelines had to be established. These were derived in the following manner. It was estimated that the top 10% would be isolated by a threshold of five or more *demands* a year and that five or more *demands* a year, given the immediate availability associated with Long Loan policies, would be likely to result in three *loans* a year. Therefore, it was decided that if a Long Loan book had three or more issues in a year, it ought to be in the Popular Loan category. The simulation results also suggested that with a one-week loan period, five demands would be likely to result in four loans. Therefore, it was ruled that if a Popular Loan book had been issued four or more times in a year, it ought to remain in the Popular Loan category—otherwise it would be demoted. These rather rough and ready rules were based on the data presented in Subsections B1 and B2 above.

The monitoring problem falls into four parts, which were tackled at Lancaster as follows:

1. *Initial Monitoring of Existing Stock.* The date due labels of the entire loanable stock of monographs were examined during the summer vacation of 1969 using the threshold of three or more loans a year on the basis of total use since the book first reached the library shelves. Trials suggested that the best procedure was to monitor a section, leaving on their fore-edges books deemed 'Popular'. These were then reprocessed as a separate procedure. Students were employed at £1 per 600 books monitored. Pamphlets and oversize pamphlets, which are separately shelved sequences, are subject to consistently low usage and so were not examined. The whole operation, involving some 70,000 books was completed by eight assistants in $2\frac{1}{2}$ days at a cost of about £110, excluding supervision. Books out on loan were examined as they were returned. In the light of this experience, some modifications have been made in later monitoring:

(a) In future, decisions will be based on use during the previous twelve months only.

(b) Since the procedures were so dependent on date due labels, it was decreed that, although new date due labels could be added, old ones should not be removed—except when the book is rebound.

(c) Because it was not possible to distinguish between original issues and renewals, both were treated as separate loans. Since a single issue and two renewals by the same person would suffice to make a book 'Popular', it was considered that this was rather too sensitive a reaction. Consequently, the Service Desk staff marked renewals with an *R* beside the date on the date stamp. Subsequently, dates with an *R* were ignored in monitoring. This reduced the sensitivity of the system. It was also, in effect, a raising of the threshold.

In a larger library it might be better not to search the entire stock to identify 'Popular' books, but rather to rely on catching them as they came back from loan. Clearly, computer-based circulation systems greatly extend the scope for monitoring.

2. *Decreasing Popularity.* At intervals, Popular Loan books need to be examined lest their popularity has declined and they should revert to Long Loan status. This was done after twelve months and is likely to continue to be done annually, because the summer vacation is a particularly convenient time. Furthermore, the timing of courses can vary within

the academic year and it might well be unwise to use periods other than the academic year. Checking is done by examining just those books with yellow spots on their spines.

3. *Increasing Popularity.*   Sometimes Long Loan books rise in popularity and should be put into the Popular Loan category. It was assumed that this would be a comparatively small problem because of the well-established obsolescence effect whereby books become *less* used not more as time passes. It was assumed that these could be found without excessive re-monitoring if:

(a) books reserved were examined,
(b) spot checks were made of books being returned from loan, and
(c) sections of the library known to be subject to increasing popularity were monitored.

In the event of a substantial general rise in demand, this could become a serious problem because these three measures are, in effect, rather makeshift substitutes for a proper re-monitoring of stock.

4. *New Books.*   There is clearly no borrowing history upon which to base decisions about loan policies where new books are concerned. All duplicates are made 'Popular' on the grounds that a duplicate should not have been bought unless they are popular. For other new titles, provisions were made:

(a) A book became Long Loan unless the person recommending its purchase also recommended that it should be placed in the Popular Loan category. The forms used for recommending books were re-designed to permit this.
(b) Subject specialist assistant librarians saw recommendations for purchase and, usually, the books at the classification stage. They were encouraged to make books 'Popular' at their discretion.

It should be stressed that the penalty for individual erroneous predictions is quite small. If a popular book is left in the Long Loan category, then there is a loss of immediate availability. If a book is placed in the Popular Loan category but is not in fact in demand, then there is a loss of convenience caused by unnecessary restriction of the loan period. However, since the book is not in demand, this inconvenience will not be very frequent. In fine, it is important that the monitoring should be fairly reliable, but it is not a very serious matter if a few books are wrongly categorised.

The alternative strategy of monitoring books as they are returned from loan had been considered. Another procedure would be to determine the loan period at the time of borrowing. This could be done very cheaply with a manual issue system—and could avoid the reprocessing of books. This idea was abandoned at Lancaster for political reasons: it was considered unsatisfactory for assistants at the Service Desk to appear to be making decisions eye-ball to eye-ball with the borrower.

Much more reliable and prompter monitoring could be achieved with a computer-aided issue system. In particular, more sophisticated decision rules could be used because more information would be available (e.g. how many *different people* used this book) and more complex decision rules used than with manual monitoring.

C3. A Variable Loan and Duplication Policy

Discussion has so far been primarily in terms of *loan* policy—with perhaps a tendency to imply that *duplication* was a separate matter. This has been partly for ease of exposition and partly because in fact the amount of duplication at the University of Lancaster Library was almost trivial before 1969. Very few duplicates were bought because considerable reliance was placed in the effectiveness of the Short Loan reserve provision and because the initiative for the purchase of duplicates tended to be left with teaching staff. Since duplicates and research material were rival alternatives for the same funds, teaching staff were to some extent motivated against the purchase of duplicates. Nor were they necessarily aware of what needed duplication. Some of the duplication, especially for older material, arose by donation—occasionally by purchasing error—and so sometimes occurred with titles that were not much in demand.

Clearer realisation during 1969 of the problems of growing demand brought greater awareness of the need for duplication and two practical steps were taken:

(a) Monies were set aside as a separate fund for the purchase of duplicates.

(b) Enquiry suggested that one reason for lack of duplication was lack of communication. The staff of the Service Desk often knew that titles needed duplicating but this information did not reach the subject specialists who were responsible for initiating orders. This was circumvented by authorising the Service Desk staff to purchase additional copies as deemed fit.

More important was the recognition that a variable loan policy ought to be a variable loan *and duplication* policy. Shortening of loan periods and duplication are indeed alternative ways of increasing immediate availability. This means that they should be considered together rather than separately.

As demand increases, so loan periods need to be shortened if immediate availability is to be maintained—but as demand gets higher and higher, this becomes less and less convenient. This is true in the case of the individual book where the loan period can be reduced to hours and also for the collection as a whole where rising demand would lead to a larger and larger proportion of the books (and therefore of borrowing) being in the shorter loan categories. This suggests that it makes sense to set a threshold for reducing the loan period and *another threshold* for acquiring another copy. On or above the *duplication threshold* another copy would be purchased. When it arrived, the demand for that *title* would be spread over *two copies*, reducing the level of demand on *each* and, thereby, reducing the need for restricted loan periods and yet increasing immediate availability. If, after the splitting of the demand, individual copies are still in such high demand that they remain above the duplication threshold, then another copy should be bought—and yet another if demand continues to warrant it until the extent of duplication has reduced the demand on *individual copies* to a more modest level.

How high these thresholds should be depends upon the Satisfaction Level sought. How high they should be in relation to each other will depend upon the relative values placed on reducing the amount of shorter period borrowing compared with other uses of the funds that duplication would consume.

In this way 'borrowing convenience', as measured by the proportion of loans (or books) subject to a shorter loan period, can be used as an additional standard of service and, in the long term, investment in duplicate copies can be objectively regulated in order to keep duplication costs at the minimum required to maintain the desired level of borrowing convenience as well as Satisfaction Level and Collection Bias.

There is a very important practical consequence of all this. By basing loan and duplication decisions on individual copies, it is possible to maintain a variable loan and duplication policy by inspecting the demand for individual documents regardless of whether or not the library also possesses other copies. If the demand on *this* copy is over the chosen threshold, then action is called for, however many other copies the library owns. This ability to monitor without establishing the number of copies owned drastically reduces the effort involved. Since the individual document reflects the demand, it will also reflect the effect of some copies going missing.

Strictly speaking, it is true that the thresholds should vary according to the number of copies held. Using the same threshold greatly increases the probability that a copy will be on the shelf as a quick calculation will demonstrate. Let us assume a desired immediate availability of 0·8 for all titles. If two copies are held and *both* monitored to achieve 0·8 immediate availability for each copy, then the probability of *neither* being on the shelf is $(1 - 0·8)(1 - 0·8) = 0·04$—or a probability of 0·96 that *a* copy is available on the shelf—i.e. an immediate availability of 96% for that title. To achieve 80% immediate availability for that title, the two copies need only have individual immediate availabilities of about 0·55. For practical purposes, this refinement is best ignored and a higher than usual immediate availability accepted where more than one copy is held. These will tend to be the books in the highest demand for which demand is most difficult to predict accurately. Consequently, the 'excessive' immediate availability constitutes a useful safety margin. In any case, it should be remembered that we are using rather crude instruments in performing these operations.

C4. Conclusion

In this section, the implementation of a variable loan and duplication policy in a library has been described. The details are particular to the University of Lancaster Library. The principles, however, appear to be generally applicable in libraries, and four other British university libraries have so far announced the adoption of a variable loan policy. It is prudent, however, to remember that a policy decision like this is likely to interact with the various technical and political ramifications of the library system. Furthermore, the introduction of computer-based circulation systems revolutionises the scope for effective stock management.

CHAPTER 8

Long-Term Implications and Self-Adaptive Control

Previous chapters have discussed ways and means of providing a better basis for determining what combination of policies can be expected to provide the best level of book availability in any given situation. However, we also know that any library situation is constantly changing. Therefore, what had seemed a good combination of policies may no longer be so. The present chapter discusses this dilemma in two parts. The first section contains a general discussion of problems of optimisation in a changing situation and stresses the need for continuing management information ('feedback'). The second section presents a theoretical analysis of the dynamics of how a variable loan and duplication policy is likely to be affected by a changing situation. In particular, such a system has highly significant properties in being able to respond and adapt to changes in the pattern of demand with minimal loss of service.

A. 'FEEDBACK' IN LIBRARIES

Any attempt to determine an optimal pattern of service to meet a given pattern of demand runs a substantial risk of failure, especially in a system like a library where the demand is rather elusive to measure and there are many subtle interactions. More specifically:

(i) The demand may have been correctly appraised but the measures taken to change provision may have been excessive, inadequate or otherwise less than optimal.

(ii) The demand may have been correctly appraised at the time but may have since changed—in which case changes in provision will cease to be optimal. In libraries, and, presumably, in other social services, changes in provision are liable in themselves to affect the demand.

(iii) The demand may have been wrongly appraised; in which case the style of provision is unlikely to be appropriate.

These problems can be largely avoided—or at least overcome—if the service is provided in a manner that is adaptive. *If* standards of performance can be developed that are a function of both demand and provision (as Satisfaction Level is), *if* the means of providing the service can be made sensitive to any mismatch between desired performance and actual performance and *if* appropriate action can then be taken, then one would be able to provide a service that is continually adapting to changes in the pattern of demand.

In library stock control, this element of adaptiveness is often absent. In very small libraries, where the librarian personally knows his stock and his users well, it is possible to maintain a library service with a high and continuing level of relevance. However, as book collections increase and the number of users grows, such informal understanding and adaptiveness becomes patchy or disappears. Consequently, with medium or large libraries, some more formal arrangements are needed—but often are non-existent. Sometimes, however, use is made of requests for books that users cannot find, of interlibrary loan requests and of suggestion boxes.

University libraries, in particular, tend to ignore the need for any formal arrangements to ensure that a relevant service is provided. The emphasis is normally on the costs of the service rather than the benefit. For example, annual reports and publicity tend to stress the amount of money being spent on the service; the cost rather than the achievement. Consequently, chronically low levels of service can and do persist unnoticed by the librarian.

Public libraries are often better organised in this respect in that provision is regularly inspected and changes made in the light of the inspection.

Two notable control devices are:

(a) 'Weeding' unused material from primary storage to allow more space for new and, hopefully, more popular material.

(b) Saturation of demand for authors in continuingly high demand. For example, if checks reveal that there is rarely any book by Ian Fleming left on the shelves, then additional titles or copies will be acquired until supply matches demand to the extent that at least one or two Fleming books are normally available.

A much more sophisticated system of stock control has been under development by Mr. A. W. McClellan for over twenty years. It evolved in theory and practice at Tottenham Public Libraries in London and Mr. McClellan is devoting his retirement to its refinement and documentation.* It is a complex combination of ratios and equations designed to ensure a consistently high standard of book accessibility within a context of limited physical and fiscal resources. A central feature is the division of the stock into numerous subject 'interest categories', which are analysed independently. For each 'interest category', the desired mean number of books on the shelves ('Shelf component') and an annual replacement rate are calculated, based on measures of:

—'Issue life': the amount of usage that a book can be expected to survive physically.
—'Reader exhaustion': the amount of time before the readers interested in this subject could be expected to have read all the books provided in that subject.
—'Bibliographical obsolescence': the tendency for books to be superseded by revised editions.

Issue life and Reader exhaustion are based on evidence of use but a square root weighting is used to increase the annual replacement rate for little used interest categories.[79] When summed across interest categories, an overall 'Shelf component' and a total book budget are produced.

An example of a predictive control system ('feedforward') has been reported from the National Lending Library for Science and Technology (now the British Library Lending Division). A regression analysis relating level of use to various attributes of books (notably subject and language) resulted in decision rules for duplication based on these attributes that could be used in ordering monographs. On account of the rapid obsolescence of science literature and delays in the supply of foreign books, it is considered that an adaptive 'feedback' control system based on actual use of individual documents would give too slow a response. The practice of the National Lending Library for Science and Technology of basing purchasing policy on unsatisfied users requests is well known.

*A description of the system has recently appeared in McClellan, A. W., *The reader, the library and the book: selected papers, 1949–1970.* London: Bingley, 1973. See especially Chapter 8.

In spite of these isolated examples, library stock control, especially in university libraries, tends to lack the important element of feedback. However, the variable loan and duplication policies described in the previous chapter can have interesting adaptive properties of practical significance.

B. THEORETICAL EXAMINATION OF THE SELF-ADAPTIVE PROPERTIES OF THE LANCASTER VARIABLE LOAN AND DUPLICATION POLICY

A particularly important feature of a variable loan and duplication policy is that it presupposes repeated monitoring at intervals to ensure that the items made subject to a shorter loan period are in fact the most popular ones. This has a significance that goes far beyond the reluctant acceptance of yet another clerical routine, because the recurrent monitoring of the stock is in effect a matter of using feedback to make the library provision continuously responsive to changes in the pattern of demand. This constitutes a self-adaptive stock control system. The mechanics of this control system require careful description.

B1. Fixed Level Threshold: No Duplication

The simplest case is where there is no duplication but where books are made, on an individual basis, subject to a shorter loan period when there is evidence that the level of demand for them rises above a fixed threshold. Not only is it true of an individual document that the loan period will become shorter as demand rises, but also of collections. If there is a continuing rise in demand for a group of books (whether a library or a part of a library), then this will be reflected by a continuing increase in the proportion of books in that group that has been made subject to a shorter loan period. A growing proportion of the borrowings from the collection will be for a shorter loan period. This may be less convenient for the borrower, but the standards of service in terms of Satisfaction Level and Collection Bias will have been largely preserved in the face of increasing demand.

Similarly, a decline in demand is likely to have a reverse effect. Just as an individual document will move to a longer loan period as the level of demand falls below the appropriate threshold, so also there will be a decline in the number (and proportion) of books subject to a shorter loan period in a class of books with a declining demand. In the long term, the reduced number of borrowers will find, to their added convenience, that less of their borrowing is for relatively short periods. Because of the decline in demand, this can be permitted without the loss of Satisfaction Level and Collection Bias.

The mechanism is depicted graphically in Fig. 8.1. This shows a hypothetical distribution of demand over titles in a library (marked

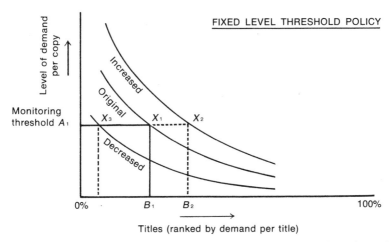

Fig. 8.1.   The effect of a fixed monitoring threshold on different levels of demand.

'original'). Because at this point we assume one copy per title, level of demand per copy is level of demand per title. A monitoring threshold set at level of demand A_1 would isolate $B_1\%$ of the library stock. The effect of an overall increase in demand is represented by the line marked 'increased'. If the monitoring threshold were to remain fixed at A_1, then the proportion of titles isolated by it would rise to B_2. Conversely, a general fall in demand, represented by the line marked 'decreased' would, on the same fixed threshold A_1, lead to a much smaller percentage of titles being isolated.

With a fixed level threshold and no duplication, an increase in demand causes the system to respond by maintaining availability at the cost of increased inconvenience to the borrower through a greater proportion of shorter loans—effectively reducing the mean loan period.

An increase in the *proportion* of shorter period loans is conveniently collected evidence of an increase in demand unaccompanied by a corresponding increase in duplication.

B2. Fixed Proportion Threshold: No Duplication

An alternative strategy would be to avoid increasing the proportion of shorter loan periods by varying the threshold used for monitoring in such a way that the proportion of titles isolated remained constant. In this case, the actual value of the threshold would have to be continuously under review.

The effect of such a policy is illustrated in Fig. 8.2. Let us consider initially the line marked 'Original'. This represents a library in which (as in

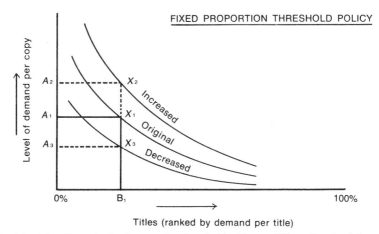

Fig. 8.2. The effect of a fixed proportion threshold policy on different levels of demand.

Fig. 8.1) a monitoring threshold set at A_1 has the effect of isolating $B_1\%$ of the titles. In the event of an increase in demand (represented by the line marked 'Increased'), then a revised monitoring threshold A_2 will be required if the proportion of titles isolated is to remain at $B_1\%$. The borrowers' convenience will be preserved with respect to the proportion of shorter period loans. Necessarily, however, the availability of all the books in the library will decline as demand rises without a corresponding increase in duplication or shortening of loan policies. Similarly, a fixed proportion threshold policy responds to a decrease in demand by maintaining the proportion of shorter period loans (at B_1). This results in higher levels of availability than in the original circumstances (see line marked 'Decreased').

In comparison with a fixed level threshold, a fixed proportion threshold policy has two practical disadvantages:

(a) Unless the procedure is entirely computer-based, the necessary collection of data to re-calculate the threshold is likely to be an inconvenient and tedious task.

(b) The most easily collected statistical data—the number of loans in each loan category—is likely to reveal little about changes in the level of demand. It is the variation in the value of the threshold that constitutes the sensitive indicator of changes in the level of demand unaccompanied by a corresponding increase in duplication—but, unfortunately, the value of the threshold is inconvenient to estimate.

With a fixed proportion threshold policy, the system responds to changes in the level of demand by preserving the proportion of loans from different loan categories at the cost of changes in availability.

B3. Duplication

In the previous two sections, it was shown how, in the absence of duplication, two different policies would respond to changes in the level of demand. To recapitulate:

(a) A fixed level threshold policy would tend to preserve availability in the event of changes in demand. This would be signalled by a change in the proportion of shorter period loans. Availability would be preserved at the cost of a reduced mean loan period.

(b) A fixed proportion threshold policy would tend to preserve the proportion of shorter period loans in the event of changes in demand. This would be signalled by a change in the actual value of the threshold. The mean loan period would be preserved at the cost of a decline in availability.

The effect of adding an extra copy of a title is to reduce the mean level of demand per copy of that title. Since monitoring is based on the level of demand per document, the effect of acquiring additional copies of a title will eventually be to bring the copies of that title below the monitoring threshold. In the case of a collection of titles subject to a stable level of demand, the acquisition of selected duplicates will not only increase availability, but also interact with the monitoring process in the following ways:

(a) With a fixed level threshold policy, duplication will tend to reduce the number and, therefore, the proportion of titles subject to a shorter loan period while the monitoring tends to keep the level of availability the same. This will be reflected in a reduction in the proportion of loans that are for shorter loan periods.

(b) With a fixed proportion threshold policy, duplication will tend to reduce the mean level of demand per copy and, therefore, increase availability while the monitoring process tends to keep stable the proportion of loans that are subject to shorter loan periods.

These reactions can be illustrated by reference to Figs. 8.1 and 8.2. An increase in demand would lead to a change from the line marked 'Original' to the line marked 'Increased'. If the vertical axis had been measured in terms of level of demand *per title*, duplication would have been irrelevant. However, because level of demand *per copy* is what matters in monitoring and because duplication of a title has the effect of reducing the level of demand per copy of that title, duplication will tend to bring the 'Increased' curve back towards the 'Original' curve even though demand *per title* remains high. With either type of threshold policy, the effect of the monitoring process is to bring about a situation similar to a return to the 'Original' level of demand. With either policy, an original level of availability, and the original proportion of shorter loan periods, and the original threshold will all be achieved again. The only difference will be that a higher level of demand is being met with the original standards of service.

Similarly, if duplication were to outstrip demand, the line of Figs. 8.1 and 8.2 would tend towards the 'Decreased' curve. This would be signalled by a decrease in the proportion of shorter loans or a reduction in the monitoring threshold according to the policy adopted.

In other words, the monitoring process and related management information (proportion of shorter period loans; threshold level) provide *a continuous and objective measure of the adequacy of duplication in relation to the chosen standards of service*. Furthermore, the actual process of monitoring indicates which titles would be suitable candidates for duplication. It may be noted that a rise in the level of demand accompanied by *adequate* duplication does not affect the proportion of shorter loan periods or the threshold level.

B4. Synthesis

On account of the conflicting objectives, a rational loan and duplication policy must be a considered compromise. For example, the change made at Lancaster in 1969 was a package based on:

(a) 86% Satisfaction Level.
(b) 8% Collection Bias.
(c) 9% of monograph stock to be subject to a one-week loan period.
(d) 70% of loans to be subject to a one-week loan policy.

These variables are not independent but interacting and based on:

(e) the distribution of demand
(f) the level of demand
(g) the size of stock
(h) the level of duplication.

which existed in 1967–1968.

If features (e)–(h) had remained static—or if they had increased proportionately and harmoniously in step together, then one could expect the standards of service (a)–(d) to be a permanent achievement. However, such proportionate and harmonious growth is not only inherently improbable but demand, in particular, had already risen faster than the others by the time the changes were implemented.

The best hope for maintaining standards of service such as (a)–(d) above lies in adopting a policy with self-adaptive properties. The most convenient of these is a fixed level threshold policy that reacts to a rise in demand by preserving availability (a and b) at the price of a temporary rise in the proportion of short period borrowing (c and d). This temporary loss of equilibrium is conveniently signalled by the rise in the proportion of short period loans (d) and is suitably remedied by an increase in the level of duplication (h). The regaining of a level of duplication adequate for the increased level of demand will be signalled by a return to the original proportion of shorter period loans (d).

Similarly, the system will respond to changes in the distribution of demand (e) and the size of stock (f), although there appears to be little prospect of changes in either of these impinging seriously on the system.

CHAPTER 9

The Lancaster Variable Loan and Duplication Policy in Practice

INTRODUCTION

In this chapter, the impact of introducing a variable loan and duplication policy will be reviewed. Given the number of assumptions and calculations made and the rather rough and ready methods of data collection and implementation in what is, after all, a complex, sensitive and dynamic system, a detailed post-mortem is difficult. Furthermore, manual data collection for analyses of this kind rapidly becomes excessively laborious. An additional disincentive to detailed analysis is that computer-aided issue systems, which are gradually becoming available, will soon permit a wide variety of complex analyses with far less effort than manual analysis.

However, sufficient analysis has been performed to provide a number of indications of the effect of the policy. It is important to remember the chronology of events.

Up to the summer of 1969: Old loan policies in force, namely
—until the end of term for undergraduate borrowing
—until the end of the Summer Term for postgraduate and staff borrowing.

Summer 1969: Initial monitoring of stock.

Session 1969–1970: Revised loan periods:
—Popular loan: one-week loan period for more heavily used books
—Long Loan: until the end of term or end of summer vacation for all other books.

Summer 1970: First annual re-monitoring.

Session 1970–1971: Popular and Long Loan as before but some books will have changed categories.

Very little monitoring was done during the sessions 1969–1970 and 1970–1971, except for the initial assignment of new books to loan categories. The Short Loan reserve collection remained substantially unchanged throughout this period.

1. INCREASE IN BORROWING

Although there was an awareness that an improved standard of service might stimulate an increase in demand, no allowance was made for this. It was predicted that if Satisfaction Level increased from 60% to 80%, then, with demand constant, one might expect an increase in borrowings as the difference was changed from frustration to success. This implied an increase of borrowing of up to 33%, but two complicating factors suggested that the increase would be less.

(i) Reservation: whereby a book is borrowed even though it was not available when initially sought.

(ii) 'Substitutability': whereby a different, substitute book is borrowed when the one originally sought is not immediately available. Very little appears to be known about this.

In both cases, frustration is not associated with a diminution of borrowing. Consequently, to the extent to which these two factors obtain, reduction of frustration will not be associated with increased borrowing.

Within a few days of the start of the first term with the revised loan policies, it was clear that there was going to be a very substantial increase in borrowing from the open shelves. (Borrowing from the Short Loan collection is excluded throughout this chapter.) In fact, the first academic session showed an increase of 97% on the previous year as is reflected in Fig. 9.1.

In fact, these figures (which include the branch library at St. Leonard's House) tend to underestimate a little the impact of the change in that they include a small percentage (< 5%) of borrowings for material (serials, parliamentary publications, pamphlets), which were outside the scope of revised loan policies. Further, examined on a term by term basis,

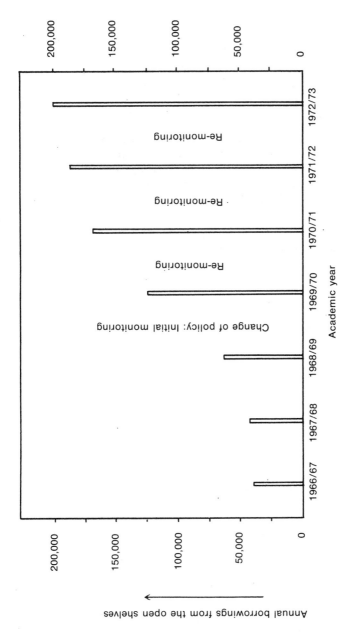

Fig. 9.1.   Annual borrowings from open shelves in successive years.

borrowings increased from term to term and during each term as it progressed, e.g.

	Borrowing from open shelves		
	1968–1969	1969–1970	Increase (%)
Autumn Term:	16,771	33,944	102%
Spring Term:	17,831	38,715	117%
Summer Term:	13,776	31,808	131%

This can best be explained by reference to the seasonal rhythm in the university. In the loan simulations, a 'steady-state' was assumed—effectively a state of continuous term with demand fixed (in the long term) and provision also fixed. However, the demand for books in a university is seasonal—punctuated in particular by the vacations and the end of examinations. Furthermore, evidence of demand is most easily seen in the borrowings, which are a function of the demand and of the availability, which is primarily determined in practice by the loan policies. Since the chronological distribution of the demand for books appears to follow a fairly stable pattern (though the *level* may vary from year to year), any given loan policy is likely to transmute the demand into a characteristic chronological pattern of borrowings.

Figure 9.2 shows the stability exhibited by borrowings in two consecutive years with the same loan periods. The data are from Lancaster in the two years preceding the change in loan policies. The whale-shaped profiles characteristic of an 'until the end of term' type policy is presumably caused by the known tendency for borrowed books to stay out until they are due back. With such a policy, the number out on loan gradually accumulates—as can be observed in the steady swelling of the loan files. Some come back but as term progresses the Satisfaction Level falls and so do borrowings—the part of demand that is satisfied. At the end of term, all books are due back and many are borrowed again by the same or other borrowers.

In contrast, a fixed period loan policy tends more quickly to a steady state—especially if the loan period is fairly short, such as a week—or shorter. The effects of longer fixed periods—such as six months—tend to be distorted by the beginnings and ends of terms. Figure 9.3 compares the 'borrowing spectrum' of Popular Loan with Long Loan. The latter is almost entirely unchanged from Long Loan in Fig. 9.2 and exhibits the same whale-shaped pattern. Popular Loan, in contrast, has flatter plateaux.

Since the revised loan policies are a combination of Popular Loan and

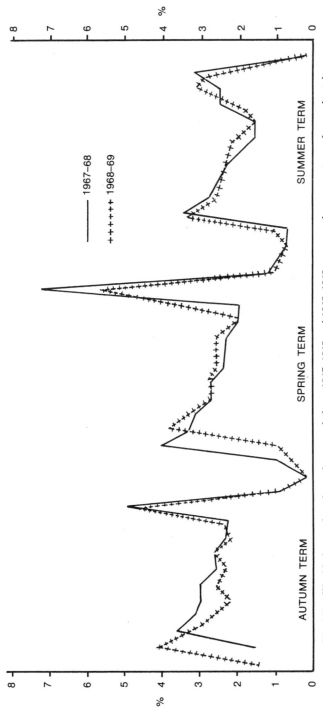

Fig. 9.2. Weekly borrowings from the open shelves, 1967–1968 and 1968–1969, expressed as percentage of annual totals. (Note that in 1967–1968 the Autumn Term was nine weeks and the Spring Term was eleven weeks instead of the normal ten. Most of the summer vacation has been omitted.)

1967–68

++++++ 1968–69

%

AUTUMN TERM

SPRING TERM

SUMMER TERM

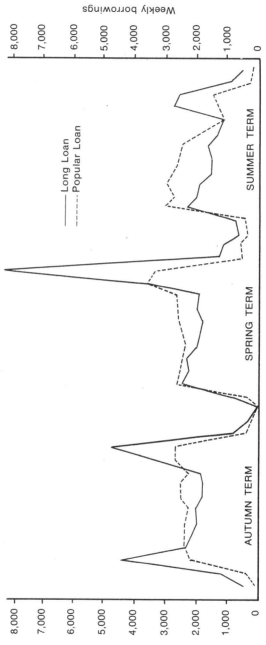

Fig. 9.3. Weekly borrowings, Long Loan and Popular Loan, from the Bailrigg Library, 1970–1971. (Most of the summer vacation has been omitted.)

Long Loan, it is only to be expected that the combined 'borrowing spectrum' should differ from that of the previous policy. One would further expect the number of borrowings with a shortish fixed period loan such as Popular Loan (or a mixture including such a loan policy) to rise relative to borrowings with an 'until the end of term' policy even though the total number of borrowings for the whole year are the same. This may account at least in part for the increase in borrowings term by term.

Normal loan periods are effectively suspended for the vacation since all books are normally borrowable for the whole vacation and there is a special incentive to borrow them at the end of term. Consequently, data on borrowings for the vacation tend to interfere with before and after comparisons: though if vacation borrowings have increased, this is partial evidence of increased demand. For example, comparisons of before and after show higher increases in issues if one compares individual weeks in term than if one compares annual borrowings.

2. PROPORTION OF ONE-WEEK LOANS

Although the proportion of stock isolated by the initial monitoring was very close to the intended 9%, the loans from Popular Loan contributed a smaller proportion of total borrowing than had been expected. The prediction had been that with perfect selection, the most popular 9% of the books on the open shelves would generate about 70% of total issues. In the event, this figure was slightly under 50%.

Random selection could be expected to achieve 9% and one explanation of the shortfall is that it reflects the less-than-perfect powers of prediction of the monitoring process used.

The small percentage of Long Loan borrowings that were from unmonitored stock and the tendency for students to stock-up for the vacation will have had a small effect in increasing Long Loan borrowings relative to Popular Loan.

3. PER CAPITA USAGE

The very substantial rise in borrowings, which is possibly unprecedented in academic librarianship, reveals a significant shift in library usage when expressed in terms of borrowing per capita. This had been fairly stable for the previous four years, around 55 borrowings per annum, if borrowing from the Short Loan reserve collection is included.

	Open shelf borrowing (per capita)	Total borrowing including reserve (per capita)
1968–1969	32	56

-----------------------------I M P L E M E N T A T I O N-------------

| 1969–1970 | 51 | 80 |
| 1970–1971 | 57 | 83 |

Strictly speaking, these figures are total borrowings divided by total student numbers (including those pursuing advanced degrees). This is somewhat misleading in that staff borrowings are included but staff are a small minority of users and their number varies closely in proportion to student numbers. The statistics given are, therefore, slightly inflated but are particularly convenient to compute and reveal the same general pattern and trends as more strictly computed statistics would.

It is clear that one effect of the revised policies was to provoke a 60% rise in open shelf borrowing per capita and that, as, with re-monitoring, the provision adapted to maintain high availability in the face of higher demand, so the users responded again with a further rise per capita of perhaps 12%. This remarkable increase in use invites a number of comments.

(i) Library usage per capita at Lancaster, as at other new universities, was already quite high to start with. Comparative data have been culled from the annual reports of 24 other libraries, mainly 1968–1969. These figures should be treated with considerable caution. The data sometimes exclude borrowings from departmental libraries and always exclude in-library use and use of neighbouring libraries: all of which may be higher than at Lancaster. Nevertheless, the figures that are summarised in Table 9.1 indicate a modal value of 15–20 issues per annum per student, but with several more in the 25–30 and 30–35 ranges. This contrasts with the values for Lancaster of 32 before implementation and subsequently 51 in 1969–1970 and 57 in 1970–1971.

(ii) Various explanations can be adduced for this increase:

(a) One possibility is that the increased borrowings represent more frequent renewals. Whilst data have not been collected on this point, there is strong evidence that in general the probability of renewal is little influenced by the length of loan period (see Chapter 6, Section B) and the subjective impression is that Lancaster is not exceptional in this respect.

(b) Another explanation is that the increase in borrowings is accounted

Table 9.1. Total Issues Divided by Number of Students (including Postgraduates) for Several British University Libraries.

Total annual issues divided by number of students (including Postgraduates)	Examples
≤ 14·9	Bath, Hull, Southampton
15·0–19·9	Bradford, Cardiff, Edinburgh, Leeds, Leicester, Nottingham, Sheffield, Newcastle
20·0–24·9	Aberdeen, Belfast
25·0–29·9	Birmingham, Bristol*, Durham, Liverpool, U.C.L., St. Andrews*, Stirling
30·0–34·9	Aberystwyth, Bristol, Dundee, *Lancaster (1968–1969)*, St. Andrews
35·0–39·9	Swansea
40·0–44·9	East Anglia*, Warwick
45·0–49·9	
50·0–54·9	East Anglia
55·0–59·9	*Lancaster (1963–1969); Lancaster (1970–1971)*
60·0–64·9	
65·0–69·9	
70·0–74·9	
75·0–79·9	
80·0–84·9	*Lancaster (1970–1971)*

*Indicates that borrowings from a 'Short Loan' or a comparable reserve collection have been excluded.

for by 'repeated borrowings', i.e. when a user borrows a book, returns it, then borrows it again later in the term when the need for it recurs. With a Long Loan period, he would probably have borrowed it once and kept it out instead of repeatedly borrowing it. Again, no data have been collected—and it would be very laborious to do so manually. This is one of a number of points that could and should be explored if a similar change of policies were to be made in a library with an automated issue system.

(c) Probably more important is the effect of the installation of the Diver Detection Device at the same time as the change in loan policies. This device is an alarm device that is activated magnetically if anyone attempts to remove a book from the library that has not been properly issued to them. Ostensibly designed to prevent theft, there was circumstantial evidence that there had been quite a lot of 'unofficial borrowing', whereby books were removed from the library and later returned—often at the end of a term. Arguably this is borrowing but it was unrecorded and the book was untraceable. Insofar as 'unofficial borrowing' was changed into recorded borrowing, there would be an increase in borrowing statistics without any real increase in usage.

Each of these factors, especially the last, probably had some effect. In the absence of data, the author believes that their effects were probably small and that the rise in borrowing represents a genuine increase in demand by the population being served in consequence of a subjective perception by them that the service is more useful and less frustrating than previously. In brief, by means of a learning process, members of the University at Lancaster have responded to change by making more intensive use of the library. It is not easy to substantiate this view, but three considerations appear to support it:

—The increase in borrowing seems to have been too massive for it to be reasonably ascribed to even the combined effects of increased renewals, repeated borrowings and the conversion of 'unofficial borrowing' into recorded borrowing.

—Increased renewals and repeated borrowings would not cause an increase in the use of material that remained on Long Loan. Yet the use of the 'unpopular' remainder increased to the extent that more borrowings were generated from these alone than there had been from *all* the books on the open shelves, namely

Autumn Term 1968:	16,771 borrowings from open shelves
Autumn Term 1969:	20,113 Long Loan
	13,831 Popular Loan

—Although the Diver Detection Device might have caused an *apparent* increase in borrowings, its installation was essentially a 'once only' event with an immediate impact. Yet re-monitoring of the stock in the summer of 1970, which was much less radical than the initial monitoring, was nevertheless followed by a further significant increase in borrowing.

(iii) Assuming that the increase in borrowing was mainly a genuine increase in demand in response to improved provision and knowing that the provision is self-adaptive to increase in demand, one wonders how long usage will continue to spiral upwards. Is the demand for library services insatiable if the service is continually raised to a very high standard? If other, older and larger universities were to implement a self-adaptive loan and duplication policy set to achieve standards of service, would the impact be even more dramatic?

4. SUBSEQUENT DEVELOPMENTS*

The substantial increase in book usage and the annual monitoring was resulting in a significant increase in the number and the proportion of books in the Popular Loan status. This increase continued even though there was also substantial purchasing of duplicates as a by-product of monitoring.

In 1970–1971, 10·9% of the monograph stock was categorised as Popular Loan and generating 47·5% of borrowing from the open shelves. In 1971–1972, this had risen to 14·1% (which was more than half again than the 9% originally intended) and was generating 53% of the borrowing from the open shelves. It was felt that this proportion was becoming inconveniently high—an excessive loss of 'borrowers convenience' in the terminology of Chapter 8, Section B. One long-term response might have been to have reduced the duplication threshold and acquired an even greater number of duplicates, but it was decided that a more immediate and a more acceptable strategy would be to raise the monitoring threshold for changing books from Long Loan status to Popular Loan status. Starting with the annual monitoring during the summer of 1972, the figure of three issues a year (excluding renewals) was changed to four issues a year (excluding renewals). This adjustment had the desired effect in that the proportion of monograph stock categorised as Popular Loan fell to 12·9% 1972–1973, though the proportion of borrowings from the open shelves fell only to 52%. Inevitably, this change will also have had an adverse effect on the Satisfaction Level and Collection Bias.

Usage, which had initially risen so dramatically, began to stabilise. Borrowing from the open shelves increased as follows.

1970–1971:	167,080
1971–1972:	186,107
1972–1973:	202,261

With an increasing user population, this indicates only a slight increase in per capita usage and was accompanied by an actual reduction in the use of the Short Loan reserve collection. In 1971–1972, there were 64 loans per capita from the open shelves and 89 including the Short Loan. In 1972–1973, this was 67 and 89, respectively.

The staff of the Library Research Unit estimate that in the middle of the academic year following the introduction of the variable loan policy (i.e.

---

*This section is based on notes kindly provided by Mr. M. Geoffrey Ford, Assistant Director of the Library Research Unit at Lancaster late in 1973. Brett et al.[237] is expected to contain a more detailed discussion.

in February 1970), the Satisfaction Level was indeed at or near 80%.* However, it was also estimated that by the Autumn Term of 1972 Satisfaction Level was down to 60%. These data are consistent with the following hypotheses:

(i) That users' demand for books is sensitive to Satisfaction Level.

(ii) That the dramatic increase in usage in 1969–1970 was a response to a sharp rise in Satisfaction Level.

(iii) That, whereas Satisfaction Level is a function of supply and demand and whereas each increase in demand reduces Satisfaction Level, successive annual monitorings have had real but relatively modest effects on Satisfaction Level (especially in 1972 when the threshold was raised) and these have been followed by modest increases in demand and usage.

The nature of the relationship between user behaviour and Satisfaction Level is not yet clear. It is possible that the relationship follows the 'learning' pattern of psychology. The idea is that the users' demand for books adapts to Satisfaction Level—and in doing so changes it. If, for example, Satisfaction Level were at, say, only 30%, users would be discouraged and demand would fall off. Assuming that the library provision does not change much, the decrease in demand will result in an increase in Satisfaction Level. As Satisfaction Level rises, so users become less discouraged and demand picks up, thus dampening Satisfaction Level. Correspondingly, if changes in library provision were to raise Satisfaction Level to, say, 90%, then the users would react very positively by using the library more. The increase in demand would reduce Satisfaction Level again (unless the library was extremely adaptable) and the lowering of the Satisfaction Level would dampen the increase in demand, probably stabilising at its new level. This 'homeostatic' theory suggests that whatever level of book availability is provided, demand will tend to adapt in such a manner that its relationship to supply tends to home in on some 'normal' satisfaction level.†

A similar but not identical theory is that the relationship between users' demand and book availability resembles that of economic theory where the demand for a product or service is 'elastic': the level of demand

---

*It is important to remember that the estimates of Satisfaction Level are only estimates and that it is not known how reliable these estimates are.

†The idea of the 'homeostatic library' is not new (see, for example, Hawgood and Morley[97], p. A3.4)—nor is speculation among library researchers that a Satisfaction Level around 60% might be a homeostatic norm for academic libraries with open access.

depends on the price—or, in this case, on a premium in the form of a perceived chance of frustration (Satisfaction Level). The lower the price—or the perceived chance of frustration (i.e. the higher the Satisfaction Level)—the higher the demand—and vice versa.

However, demand can be saturated; there is a limit beyond which people stop increasing their level of demand whatever the price—or their intensity of borrowing however high the Satisfaction Level.

Whatever precise form the relationship between book availability and users' demand may take, it is important to recognise that a dynamic relationship does seem to exist, and that it has significant implications for library management.

Part Five: Summary and Synthesis

CHAPTER 10

Summary and Synthesis

In the first part of this final chapter, the salient points of the previous nine chapters will be summarised. Then some of the disparate strands will be pulled together in an attempt to demonstrate that a synthesis of the several parts is more important than their individual significance. Finally, some concluding remarks will endeavour to relate the contents of this book to present and likely future developments in library economics.

A. SUMMARY

A1. Definition   (Chapter 1)

The purpose of a library is to make books available to people. This task is complicated by several kinds of difficulty, notably:

—the growing size and complexity of library systems;
—the large and rapidly increasing number of books published;
—the rising demand for library services;
—the varying degrees of availability in terms of convenience and immediacy;
—the diversity of purposes for which users seek books;
—the differing degrees of specificity of their demands.

The scholarly world in general has tended to concentrate on the intellectual relationships between the contents of books. This is evidenced by reviews, citations, literary criticism, and so on. Similarly the library profession has tended to concentrate heavily on the bibliographical

135

control: the use of indexes and catalogues to relate documents according to a variety of attributes, notably authorship and subject content.

The essentially logistical problem of maintaining a high standard of immediate physical availability of books has received comparatively little attention even though the problems are susceptible to theoretical, and even quantitative, analysis. Furthermore, much of the effort that has been devoted to this area has tended to concentrate on problems of storage, as reflected in the attention given to titles that are *least* used and to economical storage arrangements. This book represents a deliberate shift in emphasis. The main thrust is towards relating standards of book availability to the needs and behaviour of library users by examining the effects of activities that are critical in this relationship: acquisitions, discarding, binding, lending and duplication. Since a large amount of the demand for books tends to be concentrated on a small proportion of a library's stock, this emphasis is evidenced in the attention given to the management of titles that are in relatively high demand.

A2. The Stock of an Individual Library   (Chapter 2)

There is empirical evidence that the use of documents tends to follow certain patterns. The two patterns that are most relevant to the problem of managing library stock in order to maintain book availability in relation to the patterns of demand are:

(a) The distribution of demand over titles in a pattern usually known as Bradford's Law of scattering;
(b) The distribution of demand over time in a well-established pattern of obsolescence.

These two distributions both constitute, in the terminology of economics, laws of diminishing returns with respect to collection-building. They permit quantitative analyses of a range of important library management problems, though the use of these analyses is hindered by difficulties of data collection and by incompleteness stemming from an inadequate understanding of the behavioural response of users to changes in provision.

A3. Diagnosis of Stock Failure   (Chapter 3)

Techniques have been developed that permit the librarian to diagnose the extent to which his library service fails to meet the demands made on it. There is a brief review of three increasingly sophisticated types of method:

—the use of standards;
—the use of standardised document delivery tests;
—and the direct assessment of availability through users' own searches.

A4. Binding Arrangements   (Chapter 4)

A cost-benefit analysis of binding problems indicates that it could be worthwhile investment to pay extra for faster binding. This would lessen the time spent at the bindery and would thereby increase book availability.

A5. Loan and Duplication Problems: Individual Titles   (Chapter 5)

While a review of binding policies provides a relatively well-structured example of cost-benefit analysis of book availability problems, loan policies are both more complex and more important in this regard. The interactions between the factors involved (which necessarily include duplication policies) are reviewed. The basic relationship is seen to take the following form:

—*For any given loan period*, the chances of a copy being on the shelves when sought varies inversely with the popularity of the book. The greater the popularity, the lower the immediate availability; the less the popularity, the higher the immediate availability.
—*For any given popularity*, the length of the loan period and the immediate availability are inversely related. The longer the loan period, the lower the immediate availability; the shorter the loan period, the higher the immediate availability.
—*For any given level of immediate availability*, the popularity and the length of the loan period are necessarily also related. The greater the popularity, the shorter the loan period has to be; the less the popularity, the longer the loan period can be.
—*Duplication.* Increasing the number of copies available, like shortening the length of loan periods, increases immediate availability. To this extent it is an alternative strategy.

These relationships are described in detail because they lead to a most significant conclusion: If the library is intended to make documents available and if promptness is a virtue, then *the cardinal rule of library stock control is that both the loan period and the duplication policy should be related to the level of demand for the title and to each other.*

A quantitative analysis of these *a priori* relationships is then developed using data derived from a reserve collection. The results illustrate an important aspect of duplication: that *the marginal benefit of adding an extra copy falls off steadily as the level of immediate availability rises.* Conversely, as the level of immediate availability rises, so the cost of achieving an extra 5% immediate availability also rises. Doubling the number of copies will not double the probability that a copy will be available when sought.

There are problems in extending the analysis to the more complex situation of an open-access collection. Two alternative techniques are reviewed, and computer simulation (the 'Monte Carlo' technique) is seen as a more practical approach than the mathematical theory of queues.

A6. The Relationship between Borrowing Habits and Official Loan Regulations   (Chapter 6)

A necessary element in the use of the relationships described above is an understanding of the actual effects of official loan regulations on actual borrowing behaviour. Data were collected which, on analysis, showed quite clearly that *there is a marked tendency for borrowed books to be returned (or renewed) when they are due back and that this pattern emerges regardless of the length of the official loan period, the status of the borrower or the subject matter of the books borrowed.*

Data on the relationship between the length of the loan period and the probability of renewal indicated that the probability of renewal is affected little by the length of the official loan period.

Taken together, these findings mean that *the librarian has, in his ability to determine official loan periods, a powerful and precise control mechan- ism for influencing the availability of books in his library.*

A7. The Appraisal and Revision of Loan Regulations: A Case Study   (Chapter 7)

The ideas developed in Chapters 5 and 6 were applied to the University of Lancaster Library. The theoretical bases, data collection, policy recommendations and implementation are described in some detail. Instead of more conventional solutions, a 'variable' system was adopted on grounds of superior cost-effectiveness.* This involved both long and short loan periods. Individual books were assigned a loan period on the basis of expected demand.

A8. Long-Term Implications and Self-Adaptive Control (Chapter 8)

Important to the maintenance of standards of service is the continuous collection of information on the extent to which the system is failing to achieve these standards. Apart from isolated examples, libraries tend to be deficient in 'feedback' and in adaptive controls capable of keeping library provision responsive to changing circumstances. Variable loan and duplication policies, being based rather directly on library use, have important characteristics with respect to feedback and self-adaptive control. These, and the dynamics of how a variable policy responds to changing circumstances, are described.

A9. The Lancaster Variable Loan and Duplication Policy in Practice (Chapter 9)

The consequences of having introduced a variable loan and duplication policy at the University of Lancaster Library in 1969 are examined. The data strongly support the theory that the demand for library services is elastic (in the economic sense) in that improvements in the provision of services will increase demand. A change in the users' perception of book *availability* appears to be a particularly powerful determinant of the level of demand. At any rate, an improvement in book availability at Lancaster was followed by a dramatic increase in book usage.

B. SYNTHESIS

The theories and discoveries outlined in the preceding chapters are contributions towards a fuller understanding of the areas concerned: acquisitions, discarding, binding, lending and duplication. However, the significance of these contributions becomes far greater if it can be demonstrated that, by some process of synthesis, a consolidation of the parts becomes more important than their individual significance. It is suggested that the synthesis of the parts is both possible and important in

*Other libraries in the United Kingdom are also reported to have adopted a variable loan policy: Bath University of Technology Library, Bristol University Medical Library, Durham University Library and Sussex University Library.

two related ways: as a step towards internal consistency in library management and as a basis for developing the study of library economics.

B1. Internal Consistency in Library Stock Control

Each of the policies considered (acquisition, discarding, binding, lending and duplication) has been treated, as far as possible, in comparable terms. The costs have been expressed in monetary terms: acquisition costs, storage costs, binding costs, and so on.

The measure of service adopted has been book availability. The acquisitions, discarding, binding, lending and duplication policies were all evaluated principally, though not exclusively, in terms of book availability—in terms of the probability that the users will find what they seek when they seek it. This evaluation cannot be done completely because there are always some residual factors to be considered. The pursuit of maximum book availability is likely in practice to be mitigated by the pursuit of additional objectives, such as achieving comprehensiveness in the collections in some subject areas. There may also be political constraints within which the library administration operates and even purely logistical considerations are relevant, such as the actual availability through interlibrary loan of titles not acquired locally.

Nevertheless, it is suggested that it is not the completeness of either theory or quantification that matters but whether or not the theory or the quantification will help improve library services.

The availability of books is clearly central to library provision and, as a measure of library performance, must be taken very seriously. Since each policy area has been examined in terms of common costs and benefits, it becomes increasingly possible to achieve consistency between policies. In Chapter 2, much stress was laid on achieving the optimal *combination* of acquisition and discarding policies. Ideally one would like *all* the policies in a given library to constitute the optimal combination for the clientele that it serves. It seems most unlikely that such complete consistency will ever be achieved unless there are very drastic improvements in our comprehension of the effects of library services on users.

Nevertheless, within the areas considered in this book there seems reasonable grounds to believe that, with additional experience and study, greater internal consistency in library stock control policies will become feasible. It is hoped that we will be able to work towards policies that do not, for example, reduce our ability to serve users through failure to achieve a reasonable balance between acquiring new titles and duplicating titles already held, between duplication policies and loan policies, between duplication policies and binding policies, between discarding policies and acquisition policies, and so on. The range could be extended. For example, recent work on overdue notice policies (Baaske *et al.*[8]) and on optimal shelf-reading policies (Bookstein[17]) extend the number of areas that can be related to one another. Even without such extensions, the topics considered in this book cover a large proportion of most libraries' budgets. Therefore, even small moves towards greater internal consistency are likely to permit a significant improvement in cost-effectiveness with respect to book availability.

B2. Progress in Library Economics*

Library management studies seem to have an uneasy relationship with business management studies. A library is an organization and so the results of organizational studies ought to apply, unless special attributes of libraries would make the results misleading or inappropriate. A library is a purposive enterprise and one might expect the results of industrial administration research to be applicable. However, the library is not a commercial enterprise organised to produce monetary profits. It is a not-for-profit organization that makes services available to the institution or community that supports it. It does not charge the user directly for its services and does not attempt to make a profit.

Some recent research has surveyed groups of libraries almost as if they were groups of firms and has examined in detail trends and patterns in the size and broad distribution of budgets between materials and staff. The recent book *Economics of academic libraries* by Baumol and Marcus[13] is a good example. Some work also has been attempted on assessing the benefits derived, or at least perceived, by different groups using library services (e.g. Hawgood and Morley[97], Raffel and Shishko[181]).

One area that has not found a library parallel is the microeconomic approach to industrial management—also known as 'the theory of the firm'—which is basic to industrial economics. For present purposes, a simplified summary will suffice.† A firm uses a variety of inputs to produce a range of products (or services). The inputs include labour, capital and materials. The outputs comprise one or more products. The

*The concept of an economic theory of the library analogous to the economic theory of the firm is developed elsewhere by Buckland[53].

†This summary draws primarily on Cyert, R. M. and March, J. G. *A Behavioral Theory of the Firm*. Prentice-Hall, 1963.

firm is presumed to maximise its profit, which is the difference between income and expenditure. The activities that affect the amount of profit include deciding:

—how many different products to produce;
—how much of each product to produce;
—how much to invest in promotion as opposed to production;
—how much to invest in stocks of materials, equipment and labour;
—what pricing policy to adopt.

This has to be done in an interactive market. Competition and the nature of the market will affect both the costs of materials and the success in selling the product. Indeed, the response of the market to changes in marketing policies is a critical factor; so much so that the theory of the firm is almost a theory of markets, purporting to explain at a general level the way resources are allocated in response to the price system, which is an index of the state of the market.

How helpful it would be if the director of the library could have at his disposal the same kind of analytical tool as the theory of the firm provides for the director of the firm! Unfortunately, the theory of the firm is irrelevant and useless to the librarian, mainly because the library is not a firm and does not behave like one.

Nevertheless, recognising that a library is not a firm is not an end, but a point of departure for speculation concerning what kind of a theoretical construct would constitute an 'economic theory of the library' *analogous* to the economic theory of the firm.

The most obvious impediment to a library equivalent of the theory of the firm is the inapplicability of the basic measure of success: profit. What is needed is some comparable measure of library effectiveness.* For the

*By far the best starting point for the discussion of library performance is an article entitled 'Measuring the goodness of library services: a general framework for considering quantitative measures' by Orr[173]. In brief, Orr distinguishes two basic aspects of library 'goodness':

    (i) *Quality*: How good is the service?
    (ii) *Value*: How much good does it do?

Both quality and value are difficult to measure. However, Orr relates both to a basic flow of cause and effect: Greater *resources* are likely to result in a greater *capability* for providing library services (quality). Greater *capability* can be expected to result in greater *utilisation* although utilisation will depend very heavily on the *demand* for services (and how far the capability provided is relevant to the demand). Increased *utilisation* can be expected to result in increased *beneficial effects* (value). A perception of increased *beneficial effects* may result in increased *resources*.

Book availability, as used in this book, is clearly a measure of capability (quality): one that measures it in terms of users' demands.

sake of exploring the feasibility of such a theory, we can take book availability as a measure, since it does have merit as a partial measure of the effectiveness of a library service. The phrase 'partial measure' is used deliberately since it would be rash to argue that it is a complete measure of success of a library. It can be observed that this is also true of profit. Although it is a measure of the effectiveness of a firm that is taken very seriously, it is liable to be modified in practice by other objectives and constraints such as the security, self-fulfillment and other needs of the people involved.

Taking book availability as a measure, we can start to relate the activities and policies of the library to it:

—how many titles should be acquired;
—when to discard titles;
—what the binding policies should be;
—what loan policies to enforce;
—what duplication policies to adopt.

Just as the actual and potential purchasers of a product and their response to changes in marketing policies are crucial to industrial management, so also the actual and potential users of a library service and their behavioural response to change in provision are central to good library management—or should be.

Although these speculations are tentative, there does seem to be a *prima facie* case for attempting to develop a library equivalent of the theory of the firm.* Not only would it be very useful if achieved, but this approach would seem to be a necessary step if the study of the economics of libraries is to be taken seriously.

Although book availability has been widely used in one way or another by library researchers (e.g. Urquhart[220], Morse[155], Orr[171,172], Brookes[34] and the Lancaster Library Research Unit[52]), some other measure may well emerge in time. For example, given the elasticity of demand for library services, the *amount* of use—a measure used by Meier[148], Hamburg[92] and the Lancaster Library Research Unit[39,219]—has some merit.

Whatever the future may bring in terms of better and more cost-effective provision of library materials, it is difficult to envisage much progress without an understanding of the factors affecting book availability in relation to the library user.

*Project SCUL at Columbia University Libraries was a bold attempt at a complete modelling[63,90,91]. Even though far less complete and intended for educational purposes, the first management game developed by the Lancaster Library Research Unit appears to be the most comprehensive modelling achieved so far. It covers range of titles held, loan policies, duplication policies, and an elastic demand[39,219].

Appendixes

Appendix A: Analytical Models of the Implications of Scattering and Obsolescence

SUMMARY OF SYMBOLS

a Age at which material is sent for binding.

b Length of time taken to bind material.

B Annual budget.

c_1 Average purchase price for journal per title per annum.

c_2 Average binding cost per volume (i.e. per title per annum).

c_3 Average storage cost per volume.

c_4 Average cost per interlibrary loan.

d_1 Average delay in satisfying requests from shelves.

d_2 Average delay in satisfying requests by interlibrary loan.

D Overall average delay in satisfying requests.

e A constant: approx. 2·71828.

F Overall total cost.

i Age variable.

m Number of journal titles purchased.

M Number of volumes in library. (N.B. Volume is defined as one title per year so $M = nx$.)

n Number of journals in a subset of N.

n_i Number of monographs published i years ago, which the library possesses.

N Number of journals referred to in subject concerned.

N_i Number of monographs published i years ago.

q A Lagrangian multiplier.

r_n Number of references to the nth journal.

$r_n(x)$ Number of references to the n th journal that are more than x years old.

R_i Rate of demand for monographs published i years ago.

R_n Cumulative number of references to the 1st, 2nd, 3rd, . . . , and n th journals.

R_{n_i} Number of requests satisfied by the n_i titles held by the library and published i years ago.

R_N Total number of references to N journals.

S Number of requests satisfied.

t, t' Individual years.

U Unsatisfied demand.

V, w Discarding thresholds, i.e. level of usage at which a volume is discarded.

x Age in years.

α $1/\log(1 + \beta)$

β Scattering coefficient.

$\beta*$ Scattering coefficient modified to reflect imperfect selection.

λ Obsolescence coefficient.

μ Proportion of requests satisfied.

In 1967, Buckland and Woodburn explored analytically the relationship between scattering, obsolescence, usage and collections of serials. The results were published as *Some implications for library management of scattering and obsolescence* (University of Lancaster Library Occasional Paper, 1), 1968.[43] This appendix revises and extends that report. It should be read in conjunction with Chapter 2, which presents a less technical version of the same material and discusses the assumptions and background more fully.

The designation of the sections are those of the corresponding sections of Chapter 2.

A.   OBSOLESCENCE: THE VARIATION IN DEMAND FOR A TITLE THROUGH TIME

The fall-off of use of documents as they age has been analysed and described by numerous researchers. Cole's formulation[60] of obsolescence states that if $r_n(x)$ is the number of r_n references that are older than x years, then

$$r_n(x) = r_n e^{-\lambda x},$$

where λ is a constant characteristic of the subject area concerned and e is a constant.

B. SCATTERING: THE VARIATION IN DEMAND FROM TITLE TO TITLE

Bradford's Law of scattering, which was developed as long ago as 1934,[24] is essentially a law of diminishing returns in the use made of scientific serials. Although work in the field has concentrated on pure and applied sciences, there appears no reason to suppose that the use of serials in the social sciences and humanities would not follow the same law. Various papers have been written on Bradford's Law of scattering and the interested reader should refer to them (e.g. Refs. 29, 74, 122 and 232). One formulation, given by Leimkuhler[122], states, with slightly different notation, that if R_N references on a given subject are derived from N journal titles, then the n most productive of these journals would yield R_n references, where

$$R_n = R_N \frac{\log (1 + \beta n / N)}{\log (1 + \beta)}$$

or

$$R_n = \alpha R_N \log (1 + \beta n / N),$$

where

$$\alpha = 1/\log (1 + \beta)$$

and β is a constant characteristic of the subject field and the logarithm is to base e. This implies that the nth most productive title yields r_n references where

$$r_1 = R_1,$$

$$r_n = R_n - R_{n-1}, \qquad n > 1.$$

It should be stressed that the analyses that follow presuppose a law of diminishing returns of some kind, but any other formula for either obsolescence or scattering could have been used instead.

C. SAMPLE ANALYSES—PART I: ANALYSES THAT ASSUME THAT ALL TITLES ARE RETAINED FOR THE SAME LENGTH OF TIME

C1. Potentially Most Useful Stock Pattern

If we assume that a library can accommodate M volumes, then how many titles n, retained for x years, would give the most useful service? It is assumed that all titles are kept for the same length of time before being discarded (x years); and the definition of 'most useful' (which we retain throughout these analyses) is that 'of maximal immediate availability'— i.e. the stock that meets the largest amount of the demand falling upon the library. The problems caused by lending and the effect of duplication are considered in other chapters.

Demand is characterised by R_N references to N journals. If all N titles are acquired and retained forever, then the total unsatisfied demand is zero. Otherwise the unsatisfied demand, U, is made up of two components:

(i) The journals that are not taken: $R_N - R_n$.
(ii) The parts of journals that are taken but have been discarded at an age of x years: $R_n e^{-\lambda x}$.

Therefore, $U = (R_N - R_n) + R_n e^{-\lambda x}$.

Now if we assume that the n titles are the n most productive of the total of N, then

$$R_n = \alpha R_N \log(1 + \beta n/N),$$

where $\alpha = 1/\log(1 + \beta)$ so that

$$U = (R_N - R_n) + R_n e^{-\lambda x}$$
$$= R_N + R_n(e^{-\lambda x} - 1)$$
$$= R_N\{1 + \alpha(e^{-\lambda x} - 1)\log(1 + \beta n/N)\}$$

Now $M = nx$ so that $U = R_N\{1 + \alpha(e^{-\lambda M/n} - 1)\log(1 + \beta n/N)\}$. This function has the following shape:*

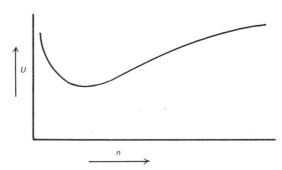

*Note that this figure is the inverse of Fig. 2.2. This figure follows the mathematics in having unsatisfied demand on the vertical scale; Fig. 2.2 follows the narrative in having satisfied demand on the vertical scale.

When we select the value of n that corresponds to the *minimal* value of U, we have the most useful stock pattern. This analysis used fundamentally the same approach as that of Cole, who produces data on scattering and obsolescence in the field of petroleum.[60] He examines the imaginary case of a petroleum library that can accommodate about 2,000 titles per year and receives 2,000 requests a year. He concludes that 190 titles, all retained for 11 years would constitute the most useful stock pattern and that this would satisfy about 75% of the requests. It should be added that in this particular case the results are not very sensitive to variations in the number of titles taken. Sixty more, or sixty fewer titles, with a corresponding adjustment to the retention period, would make little difference to the number of requests satisfied.

C2. Best Value for Money

In the previous analysis, the aim was to establish the best use of limited space: the M most useful volumes. A more practical question is how to make the best use of a limited amount of money. This is a different problem and consequently has a rather different answer.

We assume a budget of £B per annum, which must pay for:

(i) Acquisitions.
(ii) Storage (in the form of rent—or rent equivalent as interest on capital investment—light, heat and other overheads).

How many titles, n, retained for x years would give best value for money? What is the best allocation of the budget between acquisitions and storage?

Let c_1 be the average purchase cost per title per annum and c_3 be the average storage cost per volume per annum. For present purposes, a volume is defined as one title per year. Since each of the n titles is to be retained for x years,

$$B = n(c_1 + c_3 x),$$

$$n = \frac{B}{c_1 + c_3 x}.$$

Of the total demand of R_N references, we know that the number of references in the n most productive titles is R_n, where

$$R_n = \alpha R_N \log(1 + \beta n/N).$$

Since $R_n e^{-\lambda x}$ references occur after the n titles have been discarded at age x, the usefulness of the collection will be

$$R_n - R_n e^{-\lambda x} = R_n (1 - e^{-\lambda x})$$
$$= \alpha R_N (1 - e^{-\lambda x}) \log (1 + \beta n / N).$$

Substituting for n, we seek to maximise

$$\alpha R_N (1 - e^{-\lambda x}) \log (1 + \beta B / (c_1 + c_3 x) N),$$

with respect to x. The resultant values of x and n give the best policies and the effect of variations in the size of budget B can readily be calculated.

We can conveniently illustrate this analysis by calculating optimal policies for imaginary petroleum libraries. The data used by Cole, who changed his formulae to base 10 imply that when we work with Leim-kuhler's formula, the use made of a petroleum library is defined when $\beta = 256$ (when $R_N = 2,000$ and $N = 490$) and $\lambda = 0.2303$. We show below the results for two imaginary budgets for two imaginary petroleum libraries: one in central London, where storage costs are very high and one deep in the country where storage costs are very low. As in the previous analysis, the results should not be regarded as more than indicative.

	City Library	Rural Library
Assumptions:		
Annual acquisitions costs	£5 per title	£5 per title
Annual storage costs	£0·125 per volume	£0·033 per volume
Requests received	2,000 per annum	2,000 per annum
Conclusions:		
Annual budget £1,000		
Titles taken	140	175
Retention period	18 years	22 years
Volumes in stock	2520	3850
Requests satisfied	76%	80%
Annual budget £1,500		
Titles taken	205	260
Retention period	18 years	23 years
Volumes in stock	3690	5980
Requests satisfied	83%	88%

C3. Optimal Binding Policies

Although binding policies are outside the scope of this appendix, this analysis has been included because it fits neatly into the series of analyses being presented.

In this analysis, we assume binding costs must be paid from the same budget as purchase and storage costs. The problem is to determine which combination of acquisition, binding and discarding policies will give the best value for any given budget. Attention is concentrated on the two decisions: (i) when to bind; and (ii) how far it is worth paying extra for faster binding.

(i) At first sight, there is a good case for delaying binding for a while until the drop in the rate of use with time makes the temporary absence of a volume from the shelves less inconvenient to the user. Indeed, this would argue for indefinite postponement—or rather not binding at all. Until the penalty for not binding and more especially the cost of delaying binding is better understood and measured, it does not seem possible to indicate mathematically whether material should or should not be bound—still less *when* it should be bound. In the following analysis it is assumed that, as a matter of policy, titles will be bound and that material will be sent for binding at an average age of a years. The effects of choosing different values of a on the usefulness of the library can be calculated.

(ii) The time taken to bind material is defined as b years. This is the length of time that material is absent from the shelves. It is assumed that there is some choice in this matter and that although in general the cheapest binding rates will be chosen there is always the possibility of choosing to pay a little extra for a more rapid service. How far would this be justifiable?

We proceed as in the previous analysis. Let B be the annual budget, c_1 be the average purchase cost per title per annum, c_2 be the average binding cost per title per annum (N.B. The value of c_2 will depend upon the choice of binding time b, although this need not be a continuous function), and c_3 be the average storage cost per volume per annum. Therefore, since n titles are to spend b years at binding and be discarded after x years,

$$B = n(c_1 + c_2(b) + c_3 . x),$$

$$\therefore n = \frac{B}{c_1 + c_2(b) + c_3 . x}.$$

Of the total demand of R_N references, we know that the number of references in the n most productive titles is R_n, where

$$R_n = \alpha R_N \log (1 + \beta n/N).$$

The number of references satisfied before titles are sent to binding at age a is $R_n - R_n e^{-\lambda a}$. The number satisfied after a period of b years at binding will be $R_n e^{-\lambda(a+b)}$ less those lost by discarding at age x, which amount to $R_n e^{-\lambda x}$. The total usefulness of the collection will, therefore, be

$$R_n - R_n e^{-\lambda a} + R_n e^{-\lambda(a+b)} - R_n e^{-\lambda x} = R_n(1 - e^{-\lambda a} + e^{-\lambda(a+b)} - e^{-\lambda x}).$$

Substituting for n and R_n, this becomes

$$\alpha R_N(1 - e^{-\lambda a} + e^{-\lambda(a+b)} - e^{-\lambda x}) \log\{1 + \beta B/(c_1 + c_2(b) + c_3 x)N\},$$

which when *maximised* with respect to b and x denotes the best combination of policies. The effect on maximised usefulness of variations in the size of the budget B and the time of binding a can be easily determined.

To illustrate this analysis we suppose that the librarians of our imaginary petroleum libraries have three options open to them.

Binder No. 1 charges on average £1·10 per volume, but material is absent from the shelves for about three months.

Binder No. 2 charges on average £1·25 per volume, but material is absent from the shelves for one month.

Binder No. 3 charges on average £1·50 per volume but material is absent from the shelves for only about one week. (We assume one fiftieth of a year.)

We come to the same conclusions for both libraries for annual budgets of £1,000, £1,500 and £2,000. If the material is sent to binding at an average age of two years or less, then choice of binder No. 3 would, by a very narrow margin, result in the best library service even though the substantially higher cost of binding means that fewer titles can be bought. If, however, material is sent at an average age of five years, then by an even narrower margin, binder No. 2 becomes the best choice.

D.   SAMPLE ANALYSES—PART II: ANALYSES THAT DO NOT ASSUME THAT ALL TITLES ARE RETAINED FOR THE SAME LENGTH OF TIME

Investigators in this area have generally tended to assume that all titles are to be retained for the same period of time (e.g. Cole[60], Hanson[94], Meadows[147], etc.). This assumption has the great virtue of simplicity but, unless we are to deny the existence of scattering and obsolescence, it must necessarily lead to less than optimal results. In the following analyses, we determine an individual discarding age for each title: the more heavily used titles are kept longer than the less heavily used. It is assumed for simplicity that all titles in a given collection have the same obsolescence rate, but different obsolescence rates for different titles could be used if known.

D1. Potentially Most Useful Stock Pattern

If we assume that a library can accommodate only a limited number of volumes, what combination of acquisition and discarding policies would be most useful? How many titles should be purchased and for how long should each be retained?

We define r_n as the number of references to the nth title.

$$r_1 = R_1,$$

$$r_n = R_n - R_{n-1}, \qquad n > 1.$$

We do not assume that all titles are retained for the same length of time and we define x_n as the age at which the nth title is discarded. The amount of the demand for the nth title that occurs after that title has been discarded is $r_n e^{-\lambda x_n}$ so that the total satisfied demand, S, is

$$R_N - \sum_{n=1}^{n=N} r_n e^{-\lambda x_n}.$$

Since we seek the most useful stock, we seek to maximise S with respect to $x_1, x_2, x_3, \ldots, x_N$. We define M as the number of volumes that the library can hold. The restriction is, therefore,

$$\sum_{n=1}^{n=N} x_n = M.$$

(a) *Retention for Whole Years Only*

If we consider the retention policy only in terms of whole years, then $x_1, x_2, x_3, \ldots, x_N$ can only have integer values and a convenient approximation to the optimal solution can be derived as follows. Since the problem is to define the M *most useful* volumes, we would not wish to include a volume that satisfied, say, one request a year if it meant the exclusion of another volume that would have been used more than once a year. We should need, therefore, to observe the fall-off of use of each title and ensure that, at the discarding point of each, its usefulness was similar to that of the other titles. Otherwise the restriction on the number of volumes would mean that the over-prolonged retention of one title would cause the premature discarding of volumes that would have been more useful. In other words, the optimal solution is when the marginal utility of further retention is the same for all titles. We define V as the marginal rate of usefulness at which the titles are to be discarded, although since we are concerned with whole years, this can only be done approximately. The usefulness of the volume of the nth title that is x years old is

$$r_n e^{-\lambda(x-1)} - r_n e^{-\lambda x}.$$

The optimal discarding ages $x_1, x_2, x_3, \ldots, x_N$ will define the most useful volumes when for each title the age of discarding x_n is the highest value for x for which

$$r_n e^{-\lambda(x-1)} - r_n e^{-\lambda x} > V,$$

and the most useful M volumes are defined by the value of V that satisfies the condition that

$$\sum_{n=1}^{n=N} x_n = M.$$

We can profitably compare analysis C1 with this analysis. Let us re-examine the case of a petroleum library with 2,000 volumes to satisfy 2,000 requests. We find that if we accept the restriction that all titles are to be accepted for the same length of time, then at best (with about 190 titles retained for about 11 years) we could expect to satisfy 75% of the requests. If, however, as in this analysis we can choose a different retention policy for each title, then by acquiring 420 titles with retention periods varying from 1 to 23 years we can satisfy no less than 80% of the requests with 2,000 volumes.

(b) *Unrestricted Retention*

If we do not insist that only whole years are considered and $x_1, x_2, x_3, \ldots, x_N$ are not integers but continuous variables, then we can define more precisely the marginal utility of retaining each title.

$$S = R_N - \sum_{n=1}^{n=N} r_n e^{-\lambda x_n}.$$

$$\therefore \quad \frac{dS}{dx_n} = \lambda \cdot r_n e^{-\lambda x_n}.$$

Since the marginal utility is to be equalised for all titles, then we may define a variable w such that

$$\frac{dS}{dx_n} = \lambda \, . \, r_n e^{-\lambda x_n} = w, \qquad n = 1, 2, 3, \ldots, N.$$

The optimal solution is achieved when the value of w is such that the restriction

$$\sum_{n=1}^{n=N} x_n = M$$

is satisfied.

Alternatively, we can define q as a Lagrangian multiplier and define the Lagrangian function

$$S' = S + q\left(\sum_{n=1}^{n=N} x_n - M\right).$$

Then

$$\frac{dS'}{dx_n} = r_n e^{-\lambda x_n} \, . \, \lambda + q.$$

Therefore, S is maximised when

$$r_n e^{-\lambda x_n} = -q/\lambda \quad \text{and} \quad \sum_{n=1}^{n=N} x_n = M, \qquad n = 1, 2, 3, \ldots, N.$$

Both of these methods imply that each title will be retained until an age at which the remaining demand for that title is the same as the remaining demand for any other title. This would not be true if the obsolescence rate were not the same for each title.

How many titles and how long a back-set of each title should be purchased in order to establish a library that will satisfy a given percentage of demand at minimal cost? This analysis is very similar to the previous one, but introduces the concept of designing a collection to meet a specified percentage of demand instead of achieving a collection of a specified size. We assume in this analysis that the cost price per volume does not vary significantly between titles nor between years. It follows that the result would be both the most useful selection as well as the best value for money. If the costs did vary, then a more complex analysis would be needed to indicate the selection that would give the best value for money. The problem is to determine the minimal number of volumes that will satisfy the requisite proportion of requests.

The total number of requests to be satisfied is S, where

$$S = R_N - \sum_{n=1}^{n=N} r_n e^{-\lambda x_n},$$

and the collection is defined in terms of $x_1, x_2, x_3, \ldots, x_N$. Again we seek to equalise the marginal usefulness of extending each back-set further in time. This time, however, the restriction is not that the collection must reach a specified size but that the collection must satisfy a specified proportion, μ, of the demand such that

$$S = \mu R_N.$$

Consequently, we proceed as before seeking the value of V that will meet this restriction. Analysis C1 indicated that 2,000 volumes could at best satisfy 75% of demand if the restriction were accepted that all titles must be retained for the same length of time. This present analysis indicates that without this restriction, 75% of demand could be satisfied by 1,400 volumes.

D2. Optimal Library Size and Minimal Costs

If requests for items not in stock are to be satisfied by interlibrary loans, then what combination of purchasing and discarding policies will minimise library costs? We do not assume that all titles must be retained for the same length of time.

There are two methods of satisfying requests:

(i) by the acquisition and storage of titles,
(ii) by interlibrary loan.

Let c_1 be the average purchase cost per title per annum,
  c_3 be the average storage cost per volume per annum,
  c_4 be the average cost per interlibrary loan,
  F be the total overall cost,
and
  m be the number of titles purchased.

The total overall cost F will comprise four parts: the sum of the purchase costs of the m titles purchased, the sum of the storage costs of the volumes purchased and not yet discarded at age x_n, the sum of the interlibrary loan costs for requests for discarded material and the sum of interlibrary loan costs for requests for titles not acquired at all.

$$F = \sum_{n=1}^{n=m} c_1 + \sum_{n=1}^{n=m} c_3 . x_n + \sum_{n=1}^{n=m} c_4 . r_n e^{-\lambda x_n} + \sum_{n=m+1}^{n=N} c_4 . r_n.$$

The problem is to determine the values of $x_1, x_2, x_3, \ldots, x_N$ and m that minimise F.

If we consider the retention policy only in terms of whole years, then $x_1, x_2, x_3, \ldots, x_N$ can only have integer values and a convenient approximation can be achieved by examining each title and volume separately. We know the total number of requests for each title

$$r_1 = R_1,$$

$$r_n = R_n - R_{n-1}, \qquad n > 1.$$

We can also estimate the number of requests likely to fall on each volume of each title. The volume of the nth title that is x_n years old is likely to be subject to

$$r_n e^{-\lambda(x_n-1)} - r_n e^{-\lambda x_n} \qquad \text{requests.}$$

The cost of satisfying these requests by interlibrary loan would be

$$c_4\left(r_n e^{-\lambda(x_n-1)} - r_n e^{-\lambda x_n}\right).$$

It is clearly economical to retain any purchased title until the age at which its usefulness has dropped to the level at which the requests that still occur can be more cheaply satisfied by interlibrary loans than by continued storage. In other words, the best x_n is the highest value of x_n for which

$$c_4\left(r_n e^{-\lambda(x_n-1)} - r_n e^{-\lambda x_n}\right) > c_3.$$

However, in view of the cost of purchasing the title in the first place, it might still not be worth having. The number of requests that it would satisfy before being discarded is

$$r_n - r_n e^{-\lambda x_n},$$

and it would only be worth having if the cost of satisfying these requests by interlibrary loan were more than the combined cost of purchase and storage whilst retained, i.e. if

$$c_4\left(r_n - r_n e^{-\lambda x_n}\right) > c_1 + c_3 \cdot x_n.$$

The minimal cost occurs, then, when for each title we select the largest value of x_n that satisfies the condition

$$c_4\left(r_n e^{-\lambda(x_n-1)} - r_n e^{-\lambda x_n}\right) > c_3,$$

and we require only such titles as satisfy the condition

$$c_4\left(r_n - r_n e^{-\lambda x_n}\right) > c_1 + c_3 x_n.$$

The number of titles that satisfy this last condition is the optimal value of

m. Having thus determined the optimal values of $x_1, x_2, x_3, \ldots, x_N$ and m, we can calculate the costs, the size and other details of our imaginary libraries.

	City Library	Rural Library
Assumptions:		
Acquisition cost	£5 per title	£5 per title
Storage cost	£0·125 per volume	£0·03 per volume
Interlibrary loan cost	£1 per loan	£1 per loan
Conclusions:		
Titles taken	50	62
Retention range	11–24 years	16–30 years
Total volumes	744	1,230
Overall cost (F)	£1160	£1095
Satisfaction from stock	58%	63%

It might well be decided as a matter of policy deliberately to choose a solution other than that indicated above. For example, to satisfy a larger proportion from stock. If we define V as the marginal rate of usefulness, then we can substitute V for c_4 in the restrictions above and select a value for V that will result in the desired percentage of satisfaction from stock being achieved at minimal cost.

D3. The Cost of Reducing Delays

In the previous analysis, the aim was to minimise the cost of providing a library service to meet a specified level of demand and the choice between satisfaction from stock and satisfaction by interlibrary loan was solely on a basis of the cost to the library. No account was taken of the fact that there is a delay in satisfaction by interlibrary loan. On the other hand, causing library users to wait is generally regarded as undesirable. No way appears to have been devised for objectively measuring the cost to be assigned to this delay; nevertheless, the cost to the librarian of reducing the delay can be explored.

We define initially as constants: d_1 average delay in satisfying requests from stock, d_2 average delay in satisfying requests by interlibrary loan, and as a variable D overall average delay. We assume that $d_1 < d_2$ and note that D depends upon the proportion μ of requests satisfied from stock

$$D = \mu . d_1 + (1 - \mu)d_2$$
$$= d_2 + \mu(d_1 - d_2),$$

and since $d_1 < d_2$ and $0 \leq \mu \leq 1$, then $d_1 \leq D \leq d_2$ and $D \rightarrow d_1$ as $\mu \rightarrow 1$ we reduce D by increasing μ. The previous analysis has shown that the cost,

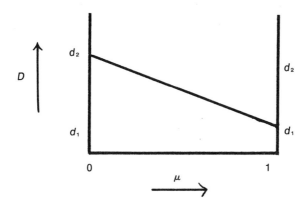

F, of supplying requests is related, under any given circumstances, to the proportion μ satisfied from stock. Assuming optimal policies, this can be calculated. As the next graph shows, F reaches a minimum when $\mu = \mu'$.

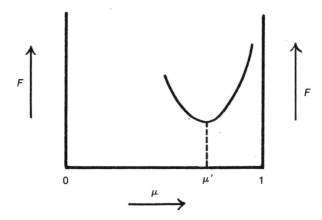

Hence, if we increase the size of the collection so that the proportion of requests satisfied from stock μ increases from 0 to μ', both average delays and unit costs are reduced. However, if we continue to increase

this proportion beyond μ' towards 1, then the continuing reduction in average delays is only achieved at the price of ever more rapidly increasing unit costs. If objective data were available on the cost to be associated with various delays, then an optimal solution could be established. Until then we can only establish the effects on average delays and on unit costs of any choice of μ, either assuming optimal policies or for any given non-optimal combination of policies, and use the information derived to help a subjective choice.

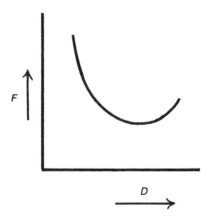

It has hitherto been assumed that the average delays d_1 and d_2 are constants. Consequently, only the effect of increasing library size was explored as a means of reducing the average delay. This is, of course, unrealistic. Even if interlibrary loans are being arranged as speedily as possible at any given unit cost, the delays can generally be reduced further at the cost of a rise in unit costs by use of telex, telephone or telefacsimile, by investing in better finding lists and union catalogues, by more or better staff, by investment in improved external lending facilities, and so on; in the extreme case, one could dispatch the enquirer by road, rail or air to another library holding the required material. It remains to be seen in any given situation how far these factors could reduce delays more economically than by increasing the size of the library.

E. MONOGRAPHS

In the preceding section and in most writings on Bradford's law, attention is confined implicitly or explicitly to serials. Although one may feel that the use of monographs *ought* to follow the same sort of pattern, the analyses presented above are not directly usable for monographs because a monograph title (unlike a serial title) is not a continuing publication.

One approach would be to treat each year's acquisitions separately and aggregate the results in the following manner.

We define

R as the rate of demand for monographs,

R_i as the rate of demand for monographs published i years ago.

Assuming that the obsolescence of monographs follows a definable pattern, we define λ as an obsolescence factor, such that

$$R_i = f(i, \lambda, R) \quad \text{and} \quad R = \sum R_i, \qquad i = 0, 1, 2, 3, \ldots.$$

We now assume that, out of a total population of N_i titles published in the year that is i years ago, a library purchased n_i. A stock comprising all N_i titles would satisfy all R_i demands but n_i, being a subset of N_i, satisfies less, R_{n_i}. Assuming that R_i (the demand for titles published in year i) were scattered over the N_i titles according to a known distribution with a scattering factor β, then if the n titles actually acquired were the n most useful titles, then

$$R_{n_i} = f(R_i, n, \beta).$$

Summing this to include the number of demands satisfied by the titles acquired in the years from t to t', the stock included would be

$$\sum_{i=t}^{i=t'} n_i$$

and the demand satisfied by this stock would be

$$\sum_{i=t}^{i=t'} R_{n_i} = \sum_{i=t}^{i=t'} f(R_i, n_i, \beta),$$

and since

$$R_i = f(i, \lambda, R),$$
$$R_{n_i} = f(i, \lambda, R, n_i, \beta),$$

and the total amount of satisfied demand would be

$$\sum_{i=t}^{i=t'} R_{n_i} = \sum_{i=t}^{i=t'} f(i, \lambda, R, n_i, \beta).$$

The utility of the stock, U, is the proportion of demand satisfied, namely

$$U = \frac{\sum_{i=t}^{i=t'} R_{n_i}}{R}.$$

It may be noted that this definition of utility—the *proportion* of demands satisfied—is independent of the actual size of the demand R. This is because both scattering and obsolescence patterns have been treated as distributions, which are not dimensional. In other words, *assuming the subject interest remains the same*, the *proportion* of the demand covered by any given collection would remain the same if the level of demand changed. The number of requests satisfied will change proportionately with the demand. This definition should not be confused with that of Brookes who has used the absolute number of requests satisfied rather than the proportion.

The model above is synchronous, i.e. it is composed by summing together the usage *at one time* of materials of many ages. However, if it is to be used dynamically—over a period of time—then it implies an understanding of the diachronous pattern, i.e. how the demand on one year's intake varies through a period of time. Morse has presented data and a model relating to the diachronous use of monographs at M.I.T. Science Library.[155] This shows the use during successive years of material acquired in one year. Morse found that the basic trend of obsolescence followed a Markov process, but that the actual usage in a year varied around the expected in a manner that could be approximated by the Poisson distribution.

A problem in this sort of approach is the difficulty of collecting adequate data by sampling techniques. However, with the development of computer-aided data processing of loan records, full details of all borrowing use becomes available, thereby greatly facilitating the study of patterns of the use of library stock. Such data only include recorded use and not unrecorded—usually 'in-library' use, but there is evidence to suggest that the distribution of 'in-library' use is the same as the distribution of 'recorded' use.[80,138] The scope for possible discrepancy between the two kinds of use varies from library to library according to the manner of provision. For example, at the University of British Columbia Library, there is little study space available inside the stacks and the data collection devices of the issue system are at the exits from the stacks. Consequently, much 'in-library' use is recorded by the computer-based issue system even though the reader merely took the book from the stacks to a reading room and did not remove the book from the library. In contrast, a fully open-access library that did not permit borrowing is likely to be particularly lacking in data on usage.

In various analyses above, it has been assumed that there is an ascertainable distribution of demand (factor β) and that when a subset of titles are acquired, n, these are the most useful titles. In practice, selection skills may well be less than ideal—especially with regard to monographs. Where the n titles acquired are not the n most useful, then clearly the actual R_n will be less than the ideal R_n. In principle, this is a measurable index of selection performance that could be reflected in a modified scattering factor, β^*. This point was noticed by Cole. An aspect of this that has not been elaborated is that for least cost optimal solutions, it may well be better to select a less useful title than a more useful title if the latter is substantially more expensive.

Appendix B: Technical Note on Predicting Demand from Incomplete Data

In Chapter 5, Subsection B1, pages 60–68, an analytical approach to the loan and duplication problems of a closed access reserve collection with fixed loan periods is presented. In the case study described, it had been possible to record data both on satisfied requests and on unsatisfied requests. More commonly, the data on unsatisfied requests are not readily available and have to be estimated.

When only data on satisfied requests are available, the problem of estimating the total number of requests (and hence the request rate) is in the following form: let us imagine the case where there are three copies of a book and we have tabulated the data on satisfied requests. If no requests were made during a loan period, then there can have been no satisfied requests, and we know from our data how often this has happened. Similarly, when one or two requests were made, and there are three copies, then all requests will have been satisfied, and, again we know the frequency of this occurrence. So far we may be confident that the total number of requests and the number of satisfied requests were the same; but the trouble begins with the remaining loan periods in which three satisfied requests have been recorded. We only know that *at least* three requests were made; we do not know on how many of these occasions there were four or more. Yet this is the crucial information: three requests could be satisfied, but if there were more, then at least one request must have gone unsatisfied. What we really need to know is the number of occasions upon which four, five, six, etc. requests were made.

However, if we are justified in assuming that, for any given item, the fluctuations in the number of requests in individual loan periods corres-

167

pond to the type of fluctuation predicted by the Poisson distribution, it is possible to estimate, from the incomplete data that we have, what the average request rate is most likely to have been. Furthermore, it is also possible to gain an impression of the amount of confidence we are entitled to place in the answer.

Since the available data include only satisfied requests, it can be tabulated as in Table B-1, where n is the number of copies, i.e. we can only observe the number of occasions f_n when n *or more* requests were made.

Table B-1.

No. of requests per loan period	Observed frequency
0	f_0
1	f_1
2	f_2
.	.
.	.
.	.
$n-1$	f_{n-1}
$\geqslant n$	f_n

If we assume that in any given loan period the actual number of requests will follow a Poisson distribution, then the likelihood of observing the tabulated data is given by

$$L = \prod_{s=0}^{n-1} \left(\frac{e^{-r}r^s}{s!}\right)^{f_s} \cdot \left[1 - \sum_{s=0}^{n-1} \frac{e^{-r}r^s}{s!}\right]^{f_n}.$$

$$\therefore \ \log L = \sum_{s=0}^{n-1} f_s \log \left(\frac{e^{-r}r^s}{s!}\right) + f_n \log \left(1 - \sum_{s=0}^{n-1} \frac{e^{-r}r^s}{s!}\right).$$

If we take a series of possible values of r, the request rate, then the corresponding values of L will indicate which value of r (the average request rate) is most likely, and will also give some indication of the extent to which this value is more likely than other possible values.* An example is given in Table B-2, where the likelihood function, L, shows a peak, albeit a rather flat one, corresponding to a request rate of 0·39. We

---

*This formula has since been used in a study of Beverly Hills Public Library: Newhouse, Joseph P. and Alexander, Arthur J. *An economic analysis of public library services.* Lexington Books, 1972. Chapter III.

Table B-2.

Data	
No. of requests per loan period	Observed frequency
0	29
1	13
$\geqslant 2$	2

Result	
r	$\log L$
0·35	− 34·39303
0·37	− 34·31419
→0·39	− 34·28505←
0·41	− 34·30062
0·43	− 34·35666

therefore conclude that 0·39 is the request rate most likely to result in the data observed. However, since this method was not necessary at Lancaster, its reliability has not been examined.

It would also seem reasonable to attempt to apply this approach to the special case of gross under-provision (when all copies are borrowed every

Table B-3.

Data	
No. of requests per loan period	Observed frequency
0	0
1	0
$\geqslant 2$	44

Result	
r	$\log L$
2	− 22·91898
4	− 4·22604
6	− 0·77016
8	− 0·13304
10	− 0·02198

loan period): What is the lowest request rate that would produce this effect? Consequently, what is the lowest number of additional copies required?

In this special case (see example in Table B-3), the likelihood function has no peak but rises to the limit of 1, and, therefore, log L to 0, as the postulated request rate rises. However, by adopting some reasonable threshold, one can at least estimate the lowest request rate likely to have produced this effect. From the data given in Table B-3 it would seem reasonable to conclude that, in this hypothetical example, the request rate is likely to have been at least six requests per loan period and that the number of copies provided should be increased accordingly.

The effort required to produce such estimates is rather oppressive in normal manual circulation systems. In the context of a computer-based circulation system, however, a little foresight and programming can generate this kind of estimate as an effortless routine.

Appendix C: Loan Data

The data presented below show how long books were kept out under a variety of loan periods.

Daily bundles of discharged slips were collected as follows:

Bristol: Data refer to items borrowed during 9–14 November 1970 and give the interval between borrowing and return. It is not known which were renewed.

Lancaster: All discharged Popular Loan slips from the main library 22 February to 6 March 1971. Note that this was after the introduction of a seven-day loan period. No distinction is made in these data between original borrowings and renewals—nor is it known whether, at the expiry of these loans, they were renewed or not—or whether they had been reserved.

Manchester: All discharged slips from the main library, 10–15 March 1969.

Strathclyde: All discharged slips from the Andersonian library, 3–15 February 1969.

Sussex: All discharged two-week loans by undergraduates from the main library, 14–27 February 1969.

The method of analysis is described in Chapter 6, Section B.

KEY:

No reservation:
  Not renewed:
    A: Time between borrowing and return.
  Renewed:
    B: Time between original borrowing and final return.
    C: Time between latest renewal and final return.

Reservation:
  Not renewed:
    D: Time between borrowing and return.
  Renewed:
    E: Time between original borrowing and final return.
    F: Time between latest renewal and final return.

(Parentheses denote science literature as defined by UDC classes 5 and 6.)

171

7-Day Loan Period

SOURCE: DAYS	BRISTOL Undergraduates	LANCASTER U/G	P/G	Staff	Others	MANCHESTER A	B	C	D	E	F
0	15	94	7	8	1	1		14			2
1	111	133	9	4	1	106		17			1
2	111	120	8	8	3	58		12	3		1
3	112	134	10	7	1	82		27	3		
4	117	134	9	12		91		36	1		
5	126	160	26	10	10	109		40	3		
6	186	413	41	14	6	160	2	64	3		3
7	581	1877	224	68	67	445	6	337	3		3
8	245	473	36	19	6	102	11	46	14		13
9	164	151	7	12	3	39	14	13	7	1	4
10	134	84	12	5	4	36	12	29	6	1	1
11	108	73	10	5	3	38	12	14	7	1	3
12	73	71	7	2	5	25	17	7	3	1	2
13	76	66	11	6	1	4	54	10	5	1	2
14	104	76	5	5	2	16	169	6		7	
15	56	17	2	3		11	34	1	1	5	1
16	28	12		1	4	7	15			2	1
17	34	16	3			3	33	3			
18	17	6		3		15	15	4	1	3	
19	9	5		2	1	5	18				
20	8	7	1			3	17			2	
21	11	6	1			6	49	1		5	1
22	12					4	17	3		3	
23	10						3	1		2	
24	12	2	1			2	7			1	
25	4					2	8			2	
26	12				1	1	9			1	
27	5	1	1		1	1	17	2	1		
28	3	2				2	22			1	
>28	171					28	130	4	4	9	1

14-Day Loan Period

SOURCE:	STRATHCLYDE: Undergraduates												SUSSEX: Undergraduates				
DAYS	A	(A)	B	(B)	C	(C)	D	(D)	E	(E)	F	(F)	A	C	D	F	DAYS
0	13	(3)			1	(1)	1	(1)					306	2			0
1	48	(17)			14	(3)	1						274	1			1
2	35	(13)			2		3	(1)					306	3			2
3	66	(20)			9	(2)	1						366	7			3
4	35	(15)			6								227	4			4
5	30	(10)			5	(2)	1						246	2			5
6	55	(19)			7	(1)	1						410	15	1		6
7	76	(26)			17	(2)	2				1	(1)					7
8	41	(17)	1		6	(1)							270	8			8
9	40	(12)			6	(3)	2	(1)					176	8	1		9
10	43	(25)			4	(2)	1				1		219	8	1		10
11	68	(23)			14	(7)	3	(1)			1		305	15			11
12	83	(26)	1		12	(4)	6	(3)			1		236	7			12
13	142	(56)			24	(12)	15	(5)					458	30	8		13
14	421	(198)	2	(1)	146	(84)	35	(15)			9	(6)	1343	115	4		14
15	91	(44)	3		21	(8)	27	(13)			4		558	39	9	1	15
16	39	(25)	1		15	(8)	4	(1)			1		210	12	5	1	16
17	60	(22)	8	(3)	10	(6)	5	(4)			2	(1)	169	13	5	1	17
18	47	(12)	3		9	(5)	6	(2)					137	16	3		18
19	44	(18)	4	(1)	14	(9)	5	(2)	1	(1)			100	6	3		19
20	49	(16)	3		7	(4)	10	(5)			2	(1)	62	3			20
21	55	(17)	12	(3)	14	(10)	6	(1)			2		120	6	1		21
22	29	(14)	5	(1)	6	(1)	4	(4)			4	(1)	63		1		22
23	14	(8)			2		1						25		1		23
24	7	(5)	8	(4)	1								44	2			24

14-Day Loan Period (*cont.*)

SOURCE:	STRATHCLYDE: Undergraduates												SUSSEX: Undergraduates				
DAYS	A	(A)	B	(B)	C	(C)	D	(D)	E	(E)	F	(F)	A	C	D	F	DAYS
25	8	(4)	8	(5)	2		2	(2)	1				30				25
26	7	(5)	9	(4)	3	(2)	1				2	(2)	30				26
27	8	(3)	31	(13)	9	(3)	3	(1)					21	1			27
28	12	(5)	63	(32)		(8)	1		8	(5)			26				28
29	1		19	(8)			2	(1)	1				13		1		29
30	3	(2)	15	(9)					1				1				30
31	1	(1)	12	(5)	1		1	(1)	1				8		1		31
32	1		8	(2)	1								21		1		32
33	2		4	(1)									4				33
34	1		6	(2)									2				34
35	2	(2)	6	(2)	1	(1)	1	(1)					10				35
36	2	(1)	3	(1)			1						1				36
37	1		5	(1)	1												37
38			3										2				38
39	1		3	(1)					1	(1)							39
40			2	(2)					1				2				40
41			2	(1)	2	(2)											41
42			9	(7)	1				1				1				42
43			2	(2)			1		1	(1)			6				43
44			1										4				44
45	2	(2)	1	(1)									4				45
46			1										6				46
47																	47
48																	48
49	1		2	(1)			1	(1)					1				49

	1696 (691)	397 (192)	396 (193)	154 (67)	30 (14)	30 (12)	6831	323	47	4
50		3 (1)						5		
51								2	1	
52		9 (3)						1		
53		4 (1)								
54		1 (1)				1				
55		5 (4)								
56		11 (8)				1				
57–63	3 (2)	21 (13)			(2)	4				
64–70	1	13 (5)								
71–77	1	19 (13)				1				
78–84	1	13 (11)								
85–91	1 (1)	8 (6)	1			2				
92–98	3 (2)	4 (2)	(1)	1	(2)	2				
99–105	1	7 (4)								
106–112	1	3 (3)								
113–119		5 (4)								
over 119		4		1 (1)	(1)	1				
Total	1696 (691)	397 (192)	396 (193)	154 (67)	30 (14)	30 (12)	6831	323	47	4

28-Day Loan Period

SOURCE: STRATHCLYDE: Staff and Postgraduates   MANCHESTER:

DAYS	A	(A)	B	(B)	C	(C)	D	(D)	E	(E)	F	(F)	A	B	C	D	E	F	A	B	C	D	E	F	DAYS
	STRATHCLYDE: Staff and Postgraduates												Postgraduates						Staff						
0	3	(1)					1	(1)																	0
1	12	(8)			4	(3)	1	(1)					2		4				5		15				1
2	7	(3)			2	(1)							10						2		13				2
3	10	(4)			4	(1)	1						5						14		15				3
4	12	(3)			2	(1)							4		2				1	1	12				4
5	17	(5)											7						1		4				5
6	15	(3)			6	(2)							4			1			3	2	2				6
7	20	(9)			2	(1)							11		4	1			12	6	3				7
8	12	(3)			4	(1)	1	(1)			1		11						3	3	10				8
9	7						1	(1)					5			1			2		4	2		1	9
10	8	(2)									1		2			1			2	1	6	2		1	10
11	11	(4)			4	(3)							5		1	1			1	3	6				11
12	9	(4)			1	(1)							6			2			2	2	15				12
13	18	(6)			3	(3)	1				3		9		1	1			2	1	14				13
14	19	(6)			2		2	(1)			3		9		3	1		1	8	3	14			1	14
15	15	(5)			2	(1)	5	(5)					3						2		9				15
16	10	(6)			2	(1)	1	(1)					3		2						2				16
17	18	(9)			2	(1)	1	(1)					6		1			1		3	15	1		1	17
18	17	(12)			2	(2)	2	(2)							1			1			9			1	18
19	13	(10)			2		2	(2)			1		2	1		1			4	4	17				19
20	16	(9)			1		3	(2)			1	(1)	2			2			2	2	11				20
21	19	(8)			3	(2)	3	(2)					9		1	1			2	3	10				21
22	12	(5)			7	(4)	5	(5)			1	(1)	7			1			2	4	6			2	22
23	20	(10)			1		1	(1)					2		3					3	5				23
24	28	(23)	1		7	(3)	2	(2)			2	(2)	4		2					8	1			1	24
25	24	(10)			20	(16)							13		2					3				2	25
26	33	(20)			12	(4)							7		7				2	4	6				26
27	52	(32)			15	(12)	3	(2)			1	(1)	10		14	2		1		3	11		1	1	27
28	**133**	**(76)**	**3**	**(1)**	**70**	**(49)**	**3**	**(3)**			**4**	**(2)**	**22**	**1**	**27**	**2**				**15**	**5**		**1**	**2**	**28**
29	32	(12)		(1)	12	(8)	7	(3)			3	(3)	12		4	1			1		5			1	29
30	16	(8)			6	(5)	3	(2)				(2)	2		4	1				4					30

31	32	33	34	35	36	37	38	39	40	41	42	43	44	45	46	47	48	49	50	51	52	53	54	55	56	57	58	59	60	61	62	63	64	65	66	67	68
1			1	1																		1															
			1		1							1															1										
	1	1																			1																
									1																												
4	3	9		1	2	5	2	9		1	4	6		1	5		7	3	6		2			1	1	3		1		1	5	3		2	1	4	2
1																1																					
			1									1							2																		
			1																			1			1												
3	3		1		1	2						1						1																			
			1			1			1	1	1			1					2	5	2		3	1	4	10	9	3	1	2	1		1			1	3
3		1	2			1	1	1				1	1								2	3				1		1									
(1)																																					
1		2																							1												
							(1)							(1)				(1)				(1)			(2)												
			1											1				1				1	1	3		1											
	(1)			(2)																																	
1	2	1	2	1		2																															
(2)	(1)	(3)	(5)	(6)		(3)	(1)					(1)											(1)	(1)	(1)									(1)			
	3	7	5	6	7	4	1	2	1		1		1			1			1						1	1	1		1								1
(2)		(2)					(2)					(1)				(4)		(1)	(5)	(2)	(7)	(15)	(3)	(3)	(2)	(1)	(2)	(1)						(1)	(1)	(4)	
2	1		1	2		2		2			1	1	2				1	5	4	2	5	5	5	2	13	22		1	3	4	3	2		1	1	4	1
(11)	(8)	(6)	(9)	(2)		(2)	(1)	(1)										(1)											(1)								
20	14	14	17	13		4	1	6	2			1				1			1										1	1							

31	32	33	34	35	36	37	38	39	40	41	42	43	44	45	46	47	48	49	50	51	52	53	54	55	56	57	58	59	60	61	62	63	64	65	66	67	68

28-Day Loan Period (cont.)

SOURCE: STRATHCLYDE: Staff and Postgraduates

	STRATHCLYDE: Staff and Postgraduates												MANCHESTER: Postgraduates						MANCHESTER: Staff						
	A	(A)	B	(B)	C	(C)	D	(D)	E	(E)	F	(F)	A	B	C	D	E	F	A	B	C	D	E	F	TOTAL
69			2	(2)							1	(1)		2											69
70			2	(1)																					70
71–77	1		8	(4)					3	(3)				3						1					71–77
78–84			14	(9)					1					6						2			2		78–84
85–91	1		15	(9)										2				1		6		1			85–91
92–98	1		15	(2)	1				2	(2)				3			1			3			1		92–98
99–105			8	(5)																					99–105
106–112	1		5	(5)					2					1						3					106–112
113–119			13	(8)																7					113–119
120–200			19	(11)	1		1	(1)	1	(1)				18			2			23		1	3		120–200
201–300	1		18	(17)	1		1		1	(1)										5			4		201–300
301–400			6	(6)																					301–400
401–500			4	(4)																1			1		401–500
501–600																				1					501–600
601–700																				1					601–700
701–800			1	(1)																					701–800
801–900			2	(2)																					801–900
TOTAL	740	(358)	244	(148)	243	(151)	62	(37)	20	(13)	20	(13)	212	94	94	20	7	7	73	235	235	10	17	17	TOTAL

Bibliography

The following bibliography represents a selection of items more or less relevant to the subject of this book. By no means all of them are referred to in the text and the interested reader is encouraged to browse through this list.

1. Allen, T. J. and Gerstberger, P. G. *Criteria for selection of an information source.* Cambridge, Mass.: M.I.T., Alfred P. Sloane School of Management, September 1967. (PB 176 899)
2. Allen, T. J. *Managing the flow of scientific and technological information.* Ph.D. thesis. Cambridge, Mass.: M.I.T., 1966. (PB 174 440)
3. Allen, T. J. *The utilization of information sources during R & D proposal preparation.* Report No. 97–64. Cambridge, Mass.: M.I.T., Alfred P. Sloane School of Management, 1964.
4. American Library Association. Library Administration Division. Section on Circulation Services. Circulation Control Committee. *Circulation policies of academic libraries in the U.S., 1968.* Chicago, Ill.: A.L.A., 1970.
5. Andrews, T. The role of departmental libraries in operations research studies in a university library. Part I. Selection for storage problems. *Special Libraries* 59, September 1968, 519–524. Part II. A statistical study of book use. *Special Libraries* 59, October 1968, 638–644.
6. Arora, S. R. and Paul, R. N. Acquisition of library materials: a quantitative approach. In: *American Society for Information Science, Proceedings, 6, San Francisco, 1969.* Westport, Conn., and London: Greenwood, 1969. Pp. 495–499.
7. Ash, L. *Yale's selective book retirement program.* Hamden, Conn.: Shoe String Press, 1963.
8. Baaske, J., Tolliver, D. L. and Westerberg, J. *Overdue policies: a comparison of alternatives.* West Lafayette, Ind.: Purdue University Libraries, 1973. (IMRU-10-73)
9. Baker, N. R. Optimal user search sequences and implications for information systems operation. *American Documentation* 20, July 1969, 203–212.

10. Barkey, P. Patterns of student use of a college library. *College and Research Libraries* **26**, March 1965, 115–118.
11. Barnikol, I. Analyse der Benutzungsfrequenz der Universitäts-und Landesbibliothek Sachsen-Arhalt in Halle/Saale. [Analysis of the frequency of use at the University and State Library of Sachsen-Arhalt, Halle/Saale], *Zentralblatt für Bibliothekswesen* **85**, 1971, 1–17.
12. Basile, V. A. and Smith, R. W. Evolving the 90% pharmaceutical library. *Special Libraries* **61**, February 1970, 81–86.
13. Baumol, W. J. and Marcus, M. *Economics of academic libraries.* Washington, D.C.: American Council on Education, 1973.
14. Beckman, M. Size and library research collections. *A[tlantic] P[rovinces] L[ibrary] A[ssociation] Bulletin* **29**, December 1965, 143–169.
15. Bobinski, G. S. Survey of faculty loan policies. *College and Research Libraries* **24**, November 1963, 483–486.
16. Bommer, M. R. W. *The development of a management system for effective decision-making in a university library*, 1972. University Microfilms Order No. 72-17328.
17. Bookstein, A. Models for shelf reading. *Library Quarterly* **43**, April 1973, 126–137.
18. Bookstein, A. and Swanson, D. R. A stochastic shelfreading model. *Library Quarterly* **43**, April 1973, 138–161.
19. Booth, A. D. On the geometry of libraries. *Journal of Documentation* **25**, March 1969, 28–42. Reprinted in: T. Saracevic (Ed.) *Introduction to information science.* New York and London: Bowker, 1970. Pp. 456–463.
20. Bourne, C. P. Some user requirements stated quantitatively in terms of the 90% library. In: A. Kent and O. Taulbee (Eds.) *Electronic information handling.* Washington, Spartan Books, 1965. Pp. 93–110.
21. Bowen, A. W. *Non-recorded use of books and browsing in the stacks of a research library.* Thesis, 1961. University of Chicago: Graduate Library School.
22. Bradford, S. C. Complete documentation. In: Royal Society Empire Scientific Conference, 1946. *Report.* London, Royal Society, 1948. Vol. 1, pp. 729–748.
23. Bradford, S. C. *Documentation.* London: Crosby Lockwood, 1948.
24. Bradford, S. C. Sources of information on specific subjects. *Engineering* **137** (3550), January 1934, 85–86. Reprinted in: P. Brophy, M. K. Buckland and A. Hindle (Eds.) *Reader in operations research for libraries.* Washington, D.C.: NCR Microcard Editions. (Forthcoming)
25. Brittain, J. M. *Information and its users: a review with special reference to the social sciences.* Bath University Press, 1970.
26. Brittain, J. M. and Line, M. B. Sources of citations and references for analysis purposes: a comparative assessment. *Journal of Documentation* **29**, March 1973, 72–80.
27. Brockis, G. J. and Cole, P. F. Evaluating the technical information function. *Chemistry in Britain* **3**, October 1967, 421–423.
28. Brookes, B. C. Bradford's Law and the bibliography of science. *Nature* **224**, December 1969, 953–955. Reprinted in: P. Brophy, M. K. Buckland and A. Hindle, (Eds.) *Reader in operations research for libraries.* Washington, D.C.: NCR Microcard Editions. (Forthcoming)
29. Brookes, B. C. The complete Bradford–Zipf 'Bibliograph'. *Journal of Documentation* **25**, 1969, 58–60.

30. Brookes, B. C. The derivation and application of the Bradford–Zipf distribution. *Journal of Documentation* **24**, December 1968, 247–265.
31. Brookes, B. C. The design of cost-effective hierarchical information systems. *Information Storage and Retrieval* **6**, June 1970, 127–136.
32. Brookes, B. C. The growth, utility, and obsolescence of scientific periodical literature. *Journal of Documentation* **26**, December 1970, 283–294.
33. Brookes, B. C. Obsolescence of special library periodicals: sampling errors and utility contours. *Journal of the American Society for Information Science* **21**, September–October 1970, 320–329.
34. Brookes, B. C. Optimum $p\%$ library of scientific periodicals. *Nature* **232** (5311), August 1971, 458–461.
35. Brookes, B. C. The optimum $p\%$ library of scientific periodicals. In: International Federation for Documentation. Study Committee 'Research on the Theoretical Basis of Information'. *Proceedings of the meeting... Moscow, 24–26 February, 1970.* Moscow: All-Union Institute for Sci. & Tech. Inf., 1970. Pp. 82–94.
36. Brookes, B. C. Photocopies v. periodicals: cost-effectiveness in the special library. *Journal of Documentation* **26**, March 1970, 22–29.
37. Brookes, B. C. Statistical distributions in documentation and library planning. In: A. G. Mackenzie and I. M. Stuart (Eds.) *Planning library services: proceedings of a research seminar, Lancaster, 1969* (University of Lancaster Library Occasional Papers, No. 3). Lancaster, England: University Library, 1969 (ED 044 153)
38. Brookes, B. C. The viability of branch libraries. *Journal of Librarianship* **2**, January 1970, 14–21.
39. Brophy, P., Buckland, M. K., Ford, G., Hindle, A. and Mackenzie, A. G. *A library management game: a report on a research project* (University of Lancaster Library Occasional Papers, No. 7). Lancaster, England: University Library, 1972.
40. Brophy, P., Buckland, M. K. and Hindle, A. (Eds.) *Reader in operations research for libraries.* Washington, D.C.: NCR Microcard Editions. (Forthcoming)
41. Brophy, P. and Buckland, M. K. Simulation in education for library and information service administration. *Information Scientist* **6**, 1972, 93–100.
42. Brown, C. H. *Scientific serials* (ACRL monograph, 16). Chicago: ACRL, 1956.
43. Buckland, M. K. and Woodburn, I. *An analytical approach to duplication and availability* (University of Lancaster Library Occasional Papers, No. 2) Lancaster, England: University Library, 1968. (ED 022 515)
    Revised versions have appeared in:

    (a) *Information Storage and Retrieval* **5**, 1969, 69–79.
    (b) T. Saracevic (Ed.) *Introduction to information science.* New York: Bowker, 1971. Pp. 193–199.

44. Buckland, M. K. Are scattering and obsolescence related? *Journal of Documentation* **28**, 1972, 242–246. Also correspondence in subsequent issue **29**, March 1973, 107–109.
45. Buckland, M. K. and Hindle, A. The case for library management games. *Journal of Education for Librarianship* **21**, 1971, 92–103.
46. Buckland, M. K. *Library stock control.* Ph.D. thesis, Sheffield University, England, 1972.
47. Buckland, M. K. Library systems and management studies at Lancaster University. In: *A world of information: proceedings of the 35th annual meeting of the American*

Society for Information Science, Washington, D.C., October 1972. Washington, D.C.:
ASIS and Westport, Conn.: Greenwood, 1973. Pp. 131–134.

48. Buckland, M. K. and Hindle, A. Library Zipf. *Journal of Documentation* **25**, March
1969, 52–57.

49. Buckland, M. K. and Hindle, A. Loan policies, duplication and availability. In: A. G.
Mackenzie and I. M. Stuart (Eds.) *Planning library services: proceedings of a research
seminar* (University of Lancaster Library Occasional Papers, No. 3). Lancaster,
England: University Library, 1969. (ED 045 173)

50. Buckland, M. K. An Operations Research study of a variable loan and duplication
policy at the University of Lancaster. *Library Quarterly* **42**, 1972, 97–106. Also in: D.
R. Swanson and A. Bookstein (Eds.) *Operations research: implications for libraries.*
Chicago: Chicago University Press, 1972. Pp. 97–106.

51. Buckland, M. K. and Woodburn, I. *Some implications for library management of
scattering and obsolescence* (University of Lancaster Library Occasional Papers, No.
1). Lancaster, England: University Library, 1968. (ED 022 502)

52. Buckland, M. K., Hindle, A., Mackenzie, A. G. and Woodburn, I. *Systems analysis of a
university library* (University of Lancaster Library Occasional Papers, No. 4). Lancaster, England: University Library, 1970. (ED 044 153)

53. Buckland, M. K. Toward an economic theory of the library. In: R. S. Taylor (Ed.)
*Symposium on the economics of information dissemination, Syracuse, 1973. Proceed-
ings.* Syracuse University Press. (Forthcoming)

54. Burkhalter, B. R. *Case studies in systems analysis in a university library.* London:
Scarecrow Press, 1968.

55. Burton, R. E. and Kebler, R. W. The 'half-life' of some scientific and technical
literatures. *American Documentation* **11**, January 1960, 18–22.

56. Cammack, F. and Mann, D. Institutional implications of an automated circulations
study. *College and Research Libraries* **28**, March 1967, 129–132.

57. Clapp, V. W. and Jordan, R. T. Quantitative criteria for adequacy of academic library
collections. *College and Research Libraries* **26**, September 1965, 371–380.

58. Clinton, M. Study of the effect of fines on circulation. *Canadian Library Journal* **29**,
May–June 1972, 248–252.

59. Cole, P. F. Analysis of reference question records as a guide to the information
requirements of scientists. *Journal of Documentation* **14**, December 1958, 197–207.

60. Cole, P. F. Journal usage versus age of journal. *Journal of Documentation* **19**, March
1963, 1–11.

61. Cole, P. F. A new look at reference scattering. *Journal of Documentation* **18**, June
1962, 58–64.

62. Colley, D. I. The storage and retrieval of stack material. *Library Association Record*
67, February 1965, 37–42, 59.

63. Columbia University Libraries. *A description of a project to study the research library
as an economic system.* New York: Columbia University Libraries, 1964.

64. Cox, J. G. *Optimum storage of library material.* Ph.D. thesis, Purdue University, 1964.

65. Danton, J. P. *Book selection and collection; a comparison of German and American
university libraries.* New York: Columbia University Press, 1963.

66. Dillehay, B. H. *et al.* Determining tomorrow's needs through today's requests: an
automated approach to interlibrary loans. *Special Libraries* **61**, May–June 1970,
238–243.

67. Duchesne, R. M. Library management information from computer-aided library

systems. In: A. G. Mackenzie and I. M. Stuart (Eds.) *Planning library services: proceedings of a research seminar, Lancaster, 1969* (University of Lancaster Library Occasional Papers, No. 3). Lancaster, England: University Library, 1969. (ED 045 173)

68. Dunn, O. C., Tolliver, D. L. and Drake, M. A. *The past and likely future of 58 research libraries, 1951–1980: a statistical study of growth and change*, 1971-72 (Ninth) issue. West Lafayette, Ind.: Purdue University Libraries, 1973.

69. Ellsworth, R. E. *The economics of book storage in college and university libraries.* Metuchen, N.J.: Scarecrow Press, 1969.

70. Ernst, M. L. and Shaffer, B. *A survey of circulation characteristics of some general library books.* Cambridge, Mass.: M.I.T., December 1954.

71. Evans, E., Borko, H. and Ferguson, P. A review of the criteria used to measure library effectiveness. *Bulletin of the Medical Library Association* 60, January 1972, 102–110.

72. Ewins, G. W. Systematic book provision. S[cottish] L[ibrary] A[ssociation] News 88, November–December 1968, 193–199.

73. Fairthorne, R. A. Algebraic representation of storage and retrieval languages. In: R. A. Fairthorne (Ed.) *Towards information retrieval.* Hamden, Conn.: Archon, 1968.

74. Fairthorne, R. A. Empirical hyperbolic distributions (Bradford–Zipf–Mandelbrot) for bibliometric description and prediction. *Journal of Documentation* 25, December 1969, 319–343. Reprinted in: T. Saracevic (Ed.) *Introduction to information science.* New York and London: Bowker, 1970. Pp. 521–534. Reprinted in: P. Brophy, M. K. Buckland and A. Hindle (Eds.) *Reader in operations research for libraries.* Washington, D.C.: NCR Microcard Editions. (Forthcoming)

75. Fairthorne, R. A. Letter. *Journal of Documentation* 25, June 1969, 152–153.

76. Fleming, T. P. and Kilgour, F. G. Moderately and heavily used biomedical journals. *Bulletin of the Medical Library Association* 52, January 1964, 234–241.

77. Ford, M. G. Data collection and feedback. In: A. G. Mackenzie and I. M. Stuart (Eds.) *Planning library services: proceedings of a research seminar, Lancaster, 1969* (University of Lancaster Library Occasional Papers, No. 3). Lancaster, England: University Library, 1969. (ED 045 173)

78. Ford, M. G. Research in user behaviour in university libraries. *Journal of Documentation* 29, March 1973, 85–106. Reprinted in: P. Brophy, M. K. Buckland and A. Hindle (Eds.) *Reader in operations research for libraries.* Washington, D.C.: NCR Microcard Editions. (Forthcoming)

79. Friis, T. The use of citation analysis as a research technique and its implications for libraries. *South African Libraries* 23, 1955, 12–13.

80. Fussler, H. H. and Simon, J. L. *Patterns in the use of books in large research libraries.* Chicago: Chicago University Press, 1969.

81. Goffman, W. and Morris, T. G. Bradford's Law and library acquisition. *Nature* 226, June 1970, 922–923.

82. Goffman, W. Mathematical approach to the spread of scientific ideas—the history of mast cell research. *Nature* 212 (5061) October 1966, 449–452.

83. Goldhor, H. (Ed.) *Research methods in librarianship: measurement and evaluation.* Champaign, Ill.: Illini Bookstore, 1968.

84. Goyal, S. K. Application of Operational Research to the problem of determining appropriate loan periods for periodicals. *Libri* 20, 1970, 94–100.

85. Goyal, S. K. A systematic method for reducing over-ordering copies of books. *Library Resources and Technical Services* 16, Winter 1972, 26–32.

86. Grant, R. S. Predicting the need for multiple copies of books. *Journal of Library Automation* **4**, June 1971, 64–71.

87. Graziano, E. G. Interlibrary loan analysis: diagnostic for scientific serials backfile analysis. *Special Libraries* **53**, May–June 1962, 251–257.

88. Grieder, E. M. The effect of book storage on circulation service. *College and Research Libraries* **9**, October 1950, 374–376.

89. Groos, O. V. Less-used titles and volumes of science journals: two preliminary notes. *Library Resources and Technical Services* **10**, Summer 1966, 289–290.

90. Haas, W. J. Computer simulation at the Columbia University Libraries. In: H. Goldhor (Ed.) *Clinic on library applications of data processing, 1964, proceedings.* Champaign, Ill.: Union Bookstore, University of Illinois, 1965.

91. Haas, W. J. Description of a project to study the research library as an economic system. In: *Association of Research Libraries, Minutes of the 63rd meeting, January 26, 1964, Chicago.* Washington, D.C.: ARL, 1964.

92. Hamburg, M., Ramist, L. E. and Bommer, M. R. W. Library objectives and performance measures and their use in decision making. *Library Quarterly* **42**, 1972, 107–128. Also in: D. R. Swanson and A. Bookstein (Eds.) *Operations research: implications for libraries.* Chicago: Chicago University Press, 1972. Pp. 107–128.

93. Hamburg, M., Clelland, R. C., Bommer, M. R. W., Ramist, L. E. and Whitfield, R. M. *A systems analysis of the library and information science data system: the research investigation, interim report to the U.S. Office of Education.* University of Pennsylvania, Philadelphia, 1970.

94. Hanson, C. W. How much space does a library need? *SIRA Technical News* **9**, 1953, 60–64.

95. Harris, I. W. *The influence of accessibility on academic library use.* Ph.D. thesis. New Brunswick, N.J.: Rutgers—The State University, 1966. (University Microfilms Order No. 67–5262.)

96. Hawgood, J. Assessing the benefits of library innovations. In: N. S. M. Cox and M. W. Grose (Eds.) *Organisation and handling of bibliographic records by computer.* Newcastle-upon-Tyne: Oriel Press, 1967. Pp. 69–71.

97. Hawgood, J. and Morley, R. *Final report on the project for evaluating the benefits from university libraries.* University of Durham Computer Unit, England, 1969. (The 'PEBUL' report.)

98. Heilprin, L. B. The economics of 'on demand' library copying. In: V. D. Tate (Ed.) *Proceedings of the eleventh annual meeting and convention,* The National Microfilm Association, Annapolis, Maryland, 1962.

99. Hillier, J. Measuring the value of information services. *Journal of Chemical Documentation* **2**, January 1962, 31–34.

100. Hindle, A. Models and measures for non-profit making services. In: A. G. Mackenzie and I. M. Stuart (Eds.) *Planning library services: proceedings of a research seminar, Lancaster, 1969* (University of Lancaster Library Occasional Papers, No. 3) Lancaster, England: University Library, 1969. (ED 045 173)

101. Hindle, A. and Buckland, M. K. Towards an adaptive loan and duplication policy for a univerity library. *O.R. Quarterly.* (Forthcoming.) Reprinted in: P. Brophy, M. K. Buckland and A. Hindle (Eds.) *Reader in operations research for libraries.* Washington, D.C.: NCR Microcard Editions. (Forthcoming)

102. Holt, C. C. and Schrank, W. E. Growth of the professional literature in economics and other fields and some implications. *American Documentation* **19**, January 1968, 18–26.

103. Houghton, B. Cut-back on periodicals. *New Library World* **73**, February 1972, 210.
104. Houghton, B. Zipf! *New Library World* **73**, November 1971, 130.
105. Humphreys, K. W. Standards in university libraries. *Libri* **20**, 1970, 144–155.
106. Iyengar, T. K. S. Circulation records in academic libraries. Data needed to assess the performance. *IASLIC Bull.* **14**, 1969, 90–96.
107. Jain, A. K. *Report on a statistical study of book use.* Lafayette, Ind.: Purdue University, Library Operations Research Project, 1967. (PB 176 525)
108. Jain, A. K. Sampling and short-period usage in the Purdue Library. *College and Research Libraries* **27**, May 1966, 211–218.
109. Jain, A. K. Sampling in-library book use. *Journal of the American Society for Information Science* **23**, 1972, 150–155.
110. Jain, A. K. *et al.* A statistical model of book use and its application to the book storage problem. *Journal of the American Statistical Association* **64** (328), December 1969, 1211–1224.
111. Kendall, M. G. The bibliography of Operational Research. *Operational Research Quarterly* **11**, May–June 1960, 31–36.
112. Kendall, M. G. Natural law in the social sciences. *Journal of the Royal Statistical Society.* Series A, 124, 1961, 1–18.
113. Kilgour, F. G. Use of medical and biological journals in the Yale Medical Library. *Bulletin of the Medical Library Association* **50**, 1962, 429–449.
114. Kovacs, H. Analysis of one year's circulation at the Downstate Medical Center Library. *Bulletin of the Medical Libraries Association* **54**, January 1966, 42–47.
115. Kozachkov, L. S. and Khursin, L. A. Osnovnoe veroyatnostnoe raspredelenie v sistemakh informatsionnykh potokov. [The basic probability distribution in information flow systems.] *Nauchno-Technicheskaya Informatsiya*, Ser. 2, 1968, No. 2, 3–12.
116. Kraft, D. H. A comment on the Morse-Elston model of probabilistic obsolescence. *Operations Research* **18**, November–December 1970, 1228–1233.
117. Kraft, D. H. and Hill, T. W. Jr. A journal selection model and its implications for librarians. *Information Storage and Retrieval* **9**, 1973, 1–11.
118. Kraft, D. H. *The journal selection problem in a university library system.* Unpublished doctoral dissertation, Purdue University, Lafayette, Ind., 1971.
119. Kujpers, J. R. Literature citation counting. *Science* **133** (3459), April 1961, 1138.
120. Lazorick, G. J. *Demand models for books in library circulation systems.* Ph.D. thesis. SUNY Buffalo, 1970.
121. Leffler, W. L. A statistical method for circulation analysis. *College and Research Libraries* **25**, November 1964, 488–490. Also Corrigenda **26**, March 1965, 144.
122. Leimkuhler, F. F. The Bradford distribution. *Journal of Documentation* **23**, September 1967, 197–207. Reprinted in: T. Saracevic (Ed.) *Introduction to information science.* New York and London: Bowker, 1970. Pp. 509–514.
123. Leimkuhler, F. F. and Cox, J. G. Compact book storage in libraries. *Operations Research* **12**, May–June 1964, 419–427.
124. Leimkuhler, F. F. A literature search and file organisation model. *American Documentation* **19**, April 1968, 131–136. Reprinted in: T. Saracevic (Ed.) *Introduction to information science.* New York and London: Bowker, 1970. Pp. 445–450.
125. Leimkuhler, F. F. *A literature search model.* Lafayette, Ind.: Purdue University, 1967. (PB 174 390)
126. Leimkuhler, F. F. Mathematical models for library systems analysis. *Drexel Library Quarterly* **4**, 1967, 185–196.

127. Leimkuhler, F. F. On information storage models. In: A. G. Mackenzie and I. M. Stuart (Eds.) *Planning library services: proceedings of a research seminar* (University of Lancaster Library Occasional Papers, No. 3). Lancaster, England: University Library, 1969. (ED 045 173)

128. Leimkuhler, F. F. *Storage policies for information systems.* West Lafayette, Ind.: Purdue University School of Industrial Engineering, Memorandum Series No. 69–8, 1969. Also in: A. G. Mackenzie and I. M. Stuart (Eds.) *Planning library services: proceedings of a research seminar* (University of Lancaster· Library Occasional Papers, No. 3). Lancaster, England: University Library, 1969. (ED 045 173)

129. Leimkuhler, F. F. Systems analysis in university libraries. *College and Research Libraries* **27**, January 1966, 13–18. Reprinted in: T. Saracevic (Ed.) *Introduction to information science.* New York and London: Bowker, 1970. Pp. 715–719.

130. Line, M. B. The ability of a university library to provide books wanted by researchers. *Journal of Librarianship* **5**, January 1973, 37–51.

131. Line, M. B. The 'half-life' of periodical literature: apparent and real obsolescence. *Journal of Documentation* **26**, March 1970, 46–54.

132. Line, M. B., Sandison, A. and Macgregor, J. *Patterns of citations to articles within journals: a preliminary test of scatter, concentration and obsolescence.* Bath, England: University Library, 1972. (BATH/LIB/2)

133. Lister, W. C. *Least cost decision rules for the selection of library materials for compact storage.* Ph.D. dissertation, Purdue University, West Lafayette, Ind., 1967. (ERIC ED 027 916)

134. Llinas, J. and O'Neill, E. T. The effect of cyclic demand on book availability. In: *American Society for Information Science, proceedings, 10, Los Angeles, 1973.* Washington, D.C.: ASIS and Westport, Conn.: Greenwood, 1973. P. 123.

135. Lubans, J. Non-use of an academic library. *College and Research Libraries* **32**, September 1971, 362–367.

136. McClellan, A. W. *The reader, the library and the book: selected papers 1949–1970.* London: Bingley, 1973.

137. McClelland, W. C. Management in a service environment. *ASLIB Proceedings* **25**, March 1973, 93–99.

138. McGrath, W. E. Correlating the subject of books taken out of and books used within an open stack library. *College and Research Libraries* **32**, July 1971, 280–285.

139. McInnis, R. M. The formula approach to library size: an empirical study of its efficiency in evaluating research libraries. *College and Research Libraries* **33**, May 1972, 190–198.

140. Mackenzie, A. G. Library research at the University of Lancaster. *Library Association Record* **73**, 1971, 90–92.

141. Mackenzie, A. G. and Stuart, I. M. (Eds.) *Planning library services: proceedings of a research seminar* (University of Lancaster Library Occasional Papers, no. 3). Lancaster, England: University Library, 1969. (ED 045 173)

142. Mackenzie, A. G. Systems analysis as a decision-making tool for the library manager. *Library Trends* **21**, April 1973, 493–504.

143. Mackenzie, A. G. Systems analysis of a university library. *Program* **2** (1), April 1968, 7–14.

144. Mackenzie, A. G. Systems analysis of a university library. In: D. J. Foskett, A. Reuck and H. Coblans (Eds.) *Library systems and information services: proceedings of the second Anglo-Czech conference of information specialists.* London: Crosby Lock-

wood, 1970. Reprinted in: P. Brophy, M. K. Buckland and A. Hindle (Eds.) *Reader in operations research for libraries*. Washington, D.C.: NCR Microcard Editions. (Forthcoming)

145. Maidment, W. R. Management information from housekeeping routines. *Journal of Documentation* 27, March 1971, 37–42.
146. Mann, S. H. Least-cost decision rules for dynamic library management. *Information Storage and Retrieval* 7, 1971, 111–121.
147. Meadows, A. J. The citation characteristics of astronomical research literature. *Journal of Documentation* 23, March 1967, 28–33.
148. Meier, R. L. Efficiency criteria for the operation of large libraries. *Library Quarterly* 31, July 1961, 215–234.
149. Meier, R. L. Information input overload: features of growth in communications—orientated institutions. In: F. Massarik and P. Ratoosh (Eds.) *Mathematical explorations in behavioral sciences*. Homewood, Ill.: Irwin, 1965, 233–273. This paper also appeared in a slightly different form in *Libri* 13, 1963, 1–44.
150. Metcalf, K. D. Is it possible to pick the ideal size for large research libraries? In: International Congress of Libraries and Documentation Centres, Brussels, 1955, *Vol. 2A: Communications*. La Haye, Nijhoff, 1955, 205–210.
151. Meyer, R. S. *Two fineless years: a history, analysis, and evaluation prepared for the Alameda County Library System, Hayward, California*. Walnut Creek, Cal.: Library Consulting Services, 1972.
152. Moreland, G. B. Operation saturation: using paperbacks, branch libraries in Maryland conduct an experiment to equate book supply with patron demand. *Library Journal* 93, May 1968, 1975–1979.
153. Morelock, M. and Leimkuhler, F. F. Library operations research and systems engineering studies. *College and Research Libraries* 25, November 1964, 501–503.
154. Morris, J. H. M. *The feasibility of using criteria book lists to evaluate Junior College Library holdings*. Ph.D. thesis. Washington State University, 1968. (University Microfilms Order-no. 68–10, 968).
155. Morse, P. M. *Library effectiveness: a systems approach*. Boston, Mass.: M.I.T., 1968.
156. Morse, P. M. Measures of library effectiveness. *Library Quarterly* 42, 1972, 15–30.
157. Morse, P. M. *On browsing: the use of search theory in the search for information* (CFSTI report AD 702 920)
158. Morse, P. M. On the prediction of library use. In: C. F. T. Overhage and R. J. Harman (Eds.) *Intrex: report of a planning conference on information transfer experiments*. Cambridge, Mass.: M.I.T., 1965. Appendix N, pp. 225–234.
159. Morse, P. M. Optimal linear ordering of information items. *Operations Research* 20, 1972, 741–751.
160. Morse, P. M. and Elston, C. A probabilistic model for obsolescence. *Operations Research* 17, January–February 1969, 36–47.
161. Morse, P. M. Search theory and browsing. *Library Quarterly* 40, October 1970, 391–408.
162. Mueller, P. H. Die Bedeutung der Bedienungstheorie im Bibliothekswesen. [The impact of queueing theory on librarianship.] *Technische Universität Dresden Wissenschaftliche Zeitschrift* 16, 1967, 1633–1636.
163. Naranan, S. Bradford's Law of science bibliography—an interpretation. *Nature* 227, August 1970, 631–632.

164. Naranan, S. Power law relations in science bibliography—a self-consistent interpretation. *Journal of Documentation* **27**, June 1971, 83–97.

165. National Libraries Committee. *Report.* London: HMSO, 1969. Cmnd 4028. Popularly known as 'the Dainton report'; Appendix C contains a discussion of closed access by E. B. Ceadel.

166. Netz, D. J. Faculty loan policies in Michigan, Ohio and Indiana. *College and Research Libraries* **30**, January 1969, 45–50.

167. Oliver, M. R. The effect of growth on the obsolescence of semi-conductor physics literature. *Journal of Documentation* **27**, March 1971, 11–17.

168. O'Neill, E. T. *Journal usage patterns and their implications in the planning of library systems.* Ph.D. thesis, Purdue University, 1970.

169. O'Neill, E. T. Limitations of the Bradford distribution. In: *American Society for Information Science. Proceedings, 10, Los Angeles, 1973.* Washington, D.C.: ASIS and Westport, Conn.: Greenwood, 1973. Pp. 177–178.

170. O'Neill, E. T. Sampling university library collections. *College and Research Libraries* **27**, November 1966, 450–454.

171. Orr, R. H. *et al.* Development of methodologic tools for planning and managing library services: II. Measuring a library's capability for providing documents. *Bulletin of the Medical Libraries Association* **56**, July 1968, 241–267. Reprinted in: P. Brophy, M. K. Buckland and A. Hindle (Eds.) *Reader in operations research for libraries.* Washington, D.C.: NCR Microcard Editions. (Forthcoming)

172. Orr, R. H. and Schless, A. P. Document delivery capabilities of major biomedical libraries in 1968: results of a national survey employing standardized tests. *Bulletin of the Medical Libraries Association* **60**, July 1972, 382–422.

173. Orr, R. H. Measuring the goodness of library services: a general framework for considering quantitative measures. *Journal of Documentation* **29**, September 1973, 315–332.

174. Page, B. S. and Tucker, P. E. The Nuffield pilot survey of library use in the University of Leeds. *Journal of Documentation* **15**, March 1959, 1–11.

175. Penner, R. J. Measuring a library's capability. *Journal of Education for librarianship* **13**, 1972, 17–30.

176. Pinzelik, B. and Tolliver, D. L. *Statistical collection simplified within the General Library.* West Lafayette, Ind.: Purdue University, Libraries and Audio-Visual Center, 1972. (IMRU-02-72)

177. Pizer, I. H. and Cain, A. M. Objective tests of library performance. *Special Libraries* **59**, November 1968, 704–711.

178. Price, D. J. de S. Citation measures of hard science, soft science, technology and nonscience. In: C. E. Nelson and D. K. Pollock, *Communication amongst scientists and technologists.* Lexington, Mass.: Heath, 1970. Pp. 3–22.

179. Price, D. J. de S. Masurari de referinte bibliografice (citate) in domeniul stiintelor dens structurate, al stiintelor slab structurate, al technicii si al stiintelor nestructurate. [Citation measures of hard science, soft science, technology and non-science.] *Studii si Cercetari de Documentare* **12**, September 1970, 205–221.

180. Pritchard, A. *Statistical bibliography: an interim bibliography.* (Report SABS-5). London: North-Western Polytechnic, School of Librarianship, 1969.

181. Raffel, J. A. and Shishko, R. *Systematic analysis of university libraries: an application of cost-benefit analysis to the M.I.T. Libraries.* Cambridge, Mass.: M.I.T., 1969.

182. Raisig, L. M. The circulation analysis of serial use: number game or key to service. *Bulletin of the Medical Libraries Association* **54**, April 1966, 104–107.

183. Raisig, L. M. Mathematical evaluation of the scientific serial. *Science* **131**, May 1960, 1417–1419.

184. Raisig, L. M. Statistical bibliography in the health sciences. *Bulletin of the Medical Libraries Association* **50**, July 1962, 450–461.

185. Ratcliffe, F. W. Manchester University Library bindery: a study of library efficiency and management. *Libri* **20**, 1970, 77–88.

186. Ratcliffe, F. W. Problems of open access in large academic libraries. *Libri* **18**, 1968, 95–111.

187. Redmond, D. A. Optimum size: the special library viewpoint. *Sci-Tech News* **20**, Summer 1966, 40–42.

188. Reichard, E. W. and Orsagh, T. J. Holdings and expenditures of U.S. academic libraries: an evaluative technique. *College and Research Libraries* **27**, November 1966, 478–487.

189. Reynolds, R. (Compiler) *A selective bibliography on measurement in library and information services.* London: Aslib, 1970.

190. Ringwalt, A. J. The *Science Citation Index*; a tool for acquiring medical serials. In: *American Society for Information Science. Proceedings, 10, Los Angeles, 1973.* Washington, D.C.: ASIS and Westport, Conn.: Greenwood, 1973. Pp. 197–198.

191. Rosenberg, V. *The application of psychometric techniques to determine the attitudes of individuals toward information seeking.* (Studies in the man-system interface in libraries, 2.) Bethlehem, Pa., Lehigh University, Center for the Information Sciences, 1966. Reprinted in: P. Brophy, M. K. Buckland and A. Hindle (Eds.) *Reader in operations research for libraries.* Washington, D.C.: NCR Microcard Editions. (Forthcoming)

192. Rosenberg, V. Factors affecting the preferences of industrial personnel for information gathering methods. *Information Storage and Retrieval* **3**, July 1967, 119–127. Reprinted in: T. Saracevic (Ed.) *Introduction to information science.* New York and London: Bowker, 1970. Pp. 95–100.

193. Ruecking, F. Selecting a circulation-control system: a mathematical approach. *College and Research Libraries* **25**, September 1964, 385–390.

194. Sandison, S. Library optimum. *Nature* **234**, December 1971, 368–369.

195. Sandison, S. The use of older literature and obsolescence. *Journal of Documentation* **27**, 1971, 184–199.

196. Saracevic, T. (Ed.) *Introduction to information science.* New York: Bowker, 1970.

197. Sewell, P. H. The evaluation of library services in depth. *UNESCO Bulletin for Libraries* **22**, November–December 1968, 274–280.

198. Seymour, C. A. Weeding the collection: a review of research on identifying obsolete stock. *Libri* **22**, 1972, 137–148 and 183–189.

199. Shaw, C. M. Duplicate provision for undergraduates. *Journal of Librarianship* **3**, July 1971, 190–206.

200. Simmons, P. *Collection development and the computer.* Vancouver: University of British Columbia, 1971.

201. Simmons, P. Improving collections through computer analysis of circulation records in a university library. In: *American Society for Information Science. Proceedings, 7, 1970.* Washington, D.C.: ASIS, 1970. Pp. 59–63.

202. Simmons, P. Reserve collections: some computer assistance for the perennial problems. *Canadian Library Journal* **29**, March–April 1972, 82–87.
203. Simon, J. L. *Economics of book storage plans for a large university library.* Ph.D. thesis, University of Chicago, 1961.
204. Simon, J. L. How many books should be stored where? An economic analysis. *College and Research Libraries* **28**, March 1967, 92–103.
205. Simon, J. L. Some principles of practical welfare economics. *Management Science* **13**, June 1967, B621–B630.
206. Slote, S. Identifying useful core collections: a study of weeding fiction in public libraries. *Library Quarterly* **41**, January 1971, 25–34.
207. Slote, S. *The predictive value of past-use pattern of adult fiction in public libraries.* Ph.D. thesis, Rutgers University, January 1969.
208. Snowball, G. J. Survey of social sciences and humanities monograph circulation by random sampling of the stack. *Canadian Library Journal* **28**, September–October 1971, 352–361.
209. Stych, F. S. Sintesi bibliografica sul Boccaccio. In: Ente Nationale Giovanni Boccaccio. *Congresso internationale tema Il Boccaccio nella cultura anglosassone.* Certaldo, 14–19 settembre 1970, Atti. (Forthcoming)
210. Trueswell, R. W. Article use and its relationship to individual user satisfaction. *College and Research Libraries* **31**, July 1970, 239–245.
211. Trueswell, R. W. Determining the optimal number of volumes for a library's core collection. *Libri* **16**, 1966, 49–60.
212. Trueswell, R. W. A quantitative measure of user circulation requirements and its possible effect on stack thinning and multiple copy determination. *American Documentation* **16**, January 1965, 20–25.
213. Trueswell, R. W. Some behavioral patterns of library users: the 80/20 rule. *Wilson Library Bulletin* **43**, 1969, 458–461.
214. Trueswell, R. W. Some circulation data from a research library. *College and Research Libraries* **29**, November 1968, 493–495.
215. Trueswell, R. W. Two characteristics of circulation and their effect on the implementation of mechanized circulation control systems. *College and Research Libraries* **25**, July 1964, 285–291.
216. Trueswell, R. W. *User behavioral patterns and requirements and their effect on the possible applications of data processing and computer techniques in a university library.* Ph.D. thesis, Evanston, Northwestern University, 1964. (University Microfilms Order No. 64-12,347.)
217. Trueswell, R. W. User circulation satisfaction vs. size of holdings at three academic libraries. *College and Research Libraries* **30**, May 1969, 204–213.
218. University Grants Committee. *Report of the committee on libraries.* London: HMSO. 1967. ('Parry report').
219. University of Lancaster. Library Research Unit. *Simulation kit no. 1. A library management game (loan and duplication policies).* Lancaster, England: University Library, 1973.
220. Urquhart, D. J. and Bunn, R. M. A national loan policy for scientific serials. *Journal of Documentation* **15**, March 1959, 21–37. Reprinted in: P. Brophy, M. K. Buckland and A. Hindle (Eds.): *Reader in operations research for libraries.* Washington, D.C.: NCR Microcard Editions. (Forthcoming)

221. Urquhart, J. A. and Schofield, J. L. Measuring readers' failure at the shelf. *Journal of Documentation* **27**, December 1971, 273–286.
222. Vickery, B. C. Bradford's law of scattering. *Journal of Documentation* **4**, 1948, 198–203.
223. Vickery, B. C. Indicators of the use of periodicals. *Journal of Librarianship* **1**, July 1969, 170–182.
224. Vickery, B. C. Periodical sets—what should you buy? *Aslib Proceedings* **5**, May 1953, 69–74.
225. Vickery, B. C. Statistics of scientific and technical articles. *Journal of Documentation* **26**, 1970, 53–54.
226. Wasserman, P. Measuring performance in a special library—problems and prospects. *Special Libraries* **49**, October 1958, 377–382.
227. Watkins, C. and Coker, N. C. Circulation policies of health science libraries. *Bulletin of the Medical Library Association* **58**, October 1970, 548–553.
228. Weber, D. C. Criteria for evaluating a college library. *Association of American Colleges Bulletin* **43**, 1957, 629–635.
229. Wessel, C. J. *Criteria for evaluating the effectiveness of library operations and services: Phase 1: Literature search and state of the art.* (ATLIS report, 10.) Washington, D.C.: John I. Thompson & Co., 1967. (AD 649 468)
230. Wessel, C. J. Criteria for evaluating technical library effectiveness. *Aslib Proceedings* **20**, November 1968, 455–481.
231. Westat Research, Inc. *A study of the characteristics, costs and magnitude of interlibrary loans in academic libraries,* Westport, Conn.: Greenwood, 1972. (Report to Association for Research Libraries.)
232. Wilkinson, E. A. The ambiguity of Bradford's law. *Journal of Documentation* **28**, June 1972, 122–130. Reprinted in: P. Brophy, M. K. Buckland and A. Hindle (Eds.) *Reader in operations research for libraries.* Washington, D.C.: NCR Microcard Editions. (Forthcoming).
233. Williams, G., Bryant, E. C., Wiederkehr, R. R. V. and Palmour, V. E. *Library cost models: owning versus borrowing serial publications, report.* Chicago: Center for Research Libraries, 1968. (NTIS PB 182 304)
234. Wood, D. N. User studies: a review of the literature from 1960 to 1970. *Aslib proceedings* **23**, January 1971, 11–23.
235. Woodburn, I. A mathematical model of a hierarchical library system. In: A. G. Mackenzie and I. M. Stuart (Eds.) *Planning library services: proceedings of a research seminar. Lancaster, 1969* (University of Lancaster Library Occasional Papers, No. 3). Lancaster, England: University Library, 1969. (ED 045 173)
236. Zipf, G. K. *Human behavior and the principle of least effort; an introduction to human ecology.* New York: Hafner, 1965.

BIBLIOGRAPHICAL POSTSCRIPT

One consequence of the impact of changed loans policies at the University of Lancaster was a renewed interest in the behavioural response of users to changes in library provision. A study entitled

'Fundamental research into factors affecting the use of library services' was undertaken with the support of the Council on Library Resources, Inc. (Grant no. 505). The results of this study are highly relevant to the contents of this book. It is planned to issue a report in 1974. The provisional citation is:

237. Brett, V. M. *et al. The academic library: a systems view.* (University of Lancaster Library Occasional Papers, No. 8). Lancaster, England: University Library. (Forthcoming) ISBN 0 901699 233.

Index